## Love-Lyrics & Songs Of Home by James Whitcomb Riley

Poet and author James Whitcomb Riley was born on October 7th 1849 in Greenfield, Indiana. Better known as the "Hoosier Poet" for his work with regional dialects, and also as the "Children's Poet" Riley was born into an influential and well off family.

However his education was spotty but he was surrounded by creativity which was to stand him in good stead later in life.

His early career was a series of low paid temporary jobs. After stints as a journalist and billboard proprietor he had the resources to dedicate more of his efforts to writing.

Riley was prone to drink which was to affect his health and later his career but after a slow start and a lot of submissions he began to gain traction first in newspapers and then with the publication of his dialect poems 'Boone County Poems' he came to national recognition. This propelled him to long term contracts to perform on speaking circuits. These were very successful but over the years his star waned.

In 1888 he was too drunk to perform and the ensuing publicity made everything seem very bleak for a while. However he overcame that and managed to re-negotiate his contracts so that he received his rightful share of the income and his wealth thereafter increased very quickly.

A bachelor, Riley seems to have his writings as his only outlet, and although in his public performances he was well received, his publications were becoming seen as banal and repetitive and sales of these later works began to fall away.

Eventually after his last tour in 1895 he retired to spend his final years in Indianapolis writing patriotic poetry.

Now in poor health, weakened by years of heavy drinking, Riley, the Hoosier Poet died on July 23, 1916 of a stroke. In a final, unusual tribute, Riley lay in state for a day in the Indiana Statehouse, where thousands came to pay their respects. Not since Lincoln had a public personage received such a send-off. He is buried at Crown Hill Cemetery in Indianapolis.


**INSCRIBED**

TO THE ELECT OF LOVE, OR SIDE-BY-SIDE
IN RAPTEST ECSTASY, OR SUNDERED WIDE
BY SEAS THAT BEAR NO MESSAGE TO OR FRO
BETWEEN THE LOVED AND LOST OF LONG AGO.

So were I but a minstrel, deft
At weaving, with the trembling strings
Of my glad harp, the warp and weft
Of rondels such as rapture sings,
I'd loop my lyre across my breast,
Nor stay me till my knee found rest
In midnight banks of bud and flower
Beneath my lady's lattice-bower.

And there, drenched with the teary dews,
I'd woo her with such wondrous art
As well might stanch the songs that ooze
Out of the mockbird's breaking heart;
So light, so tender, and so sweet
Should be the words I would repeat,
Her casement, on my gradual sight,
Would blossom as a lily might.

## Index OF Poems
### LOVE LYRICS
AN OLD SWEETHEART OF MINE
A' OLD PLAYED-OUT SONG
A VERY YOUTHFUL AFFAIR
AN OUT-WORN SAPPHO
THE PASSING OF A HEART
"DREAM"
HE CALLED HER IN
HER FACE AND BROW
HER BEAUTIFUL EYES
WHEN SHE COMES HOME
LET US FORGET
LEONAINIE
HER WAITING FACE
THE OLD YEAR AND THE NEW
THEIR SWEET SORROW
JUDITH
HE AND I
THE LOST PATH
MY BRIDE THAT IS TO BE
HOW IT HAPPENED
WHEN MY DREAMS COME TRUE
NOTHIN' TO SAY
IKE WALTON'S PRAYER
ILLILEO
THE WIFE-BLESSÉD
MY MARY
HOME AT NIGHT
WHEN LIDE MARRIED HIM
HER HAIR
LAST NIGHT - AND THIS
A DISCOURAGING MODEL
SUSPENSE
THE RIVAL
TOM VAN ARDEN
TO HEAR HER SING
A VARIATION
WHERE SHALL WE LAND?
THE TOUCHES OF HER HANDS

FARMER WHIPPLE - BACHELOR
THE ROSE
WHEN AGE COMES ON
HAS SHE FORGOTTEN?
BLOOMS OF MAY
THE SERMON OF THE ROSE

## SONGS OF HOME
WE MUST GET HOME
JUST TO BE GOOD
MY FRIEND
THINKIN' BACK
NOT ALWAYS GLAD WHEN WE SMILE
HIS ROOM
THE PLAINT HUMAN
THE QUEST
THE MULBERRY TREE
FOR YOU
A FEEL IN THE CHRIS'MAS-AIR
AS CREATED
WHERE-AWAY
DREAMER, SAY
OUR OWN
THE OLD TRUNDLE-BED
WHO BIDES HIS TIME
NATURAL PERVERSITIES
A SCRAWL
WRITIN' BACK TO THE HOME-FOLKS
LAUGHTER HOLDING BOTH HIS SIDES
THE SONG OF YESTERDAY
SONG OF PARTING
OUR KIND OF A MAN
"HOW DID YOU REST, LAST NIGHT?"
OUT OF THE HITHERWHERE
JACK-IN-THE-BOX
THE BOYS
IT'S GOT TO BE
"OUT OF REACH?"
"A BRAVE REFRAIN"
IN THE EVENING
JIM
THE BEST IS GOOD ENOUGH
HONEY DRIPPING FROM THE COMB
AS MY UNCLE USED TO SAY
WE MUST BELIEVE
A GOOD MAN
THE OLD DAYS
A SPRING SONG AND A LATER
KNEELING WITH HERRICK
THE RAINY MORNING
REACH YOUR HAND TO ME

TO MY OLD FRIEND, WILLIAM LEACHMAN
A BACKWARD LOOK
AT SEA
THE OLD GUITAR
JOHN McKEEN
THROUGH SLEEPY-LAND
"THEM OLD CHEERY WORDS"
TO THE JUDGE
OUR BOYHOOD HAUNTS
MY DANCIN'-DAYS IS OVER
HER BEAUTIFUL HANDS

James Whitcomb Riley – A Short Biography


## Love Lyrics

### AN OLD SWEETHEART OF MINE

As one who cons at evening o'er an album all alone,
And muses on the faces of the friends that he has known,
So I turn the leaves of fancy till, in shadowy design,
I find the smiling features of an old sweetheart of mine.

The lamplight seems to glimmer with a flicker of surprise,
As I turn it low to rest me of the dazzle in my eyes,
And light my pipe in silence, save a sigh that seems to yoke
Its fate with my tobacco and to vanish with the smoke.

Tis a fragrant retrospection, for the loving thoughts that start
Into being are like perfume from the blossom of the heart;
And to dream the old dreams over is a luxury divine
When my truant fancy wanders with that old sweetheart of mine.

Though I hear, beneath my study, like a fluttering of wings,
The voices of my children, and the mother as she sings,
I feel no twinge of conscience to deny me any theme
When Care has cast her anchor in the harbor of a dream.

In fact, to speak in earnest, I believe it adds a charm
To spice the good a trifle with a little dust of harm
For I find an extra flavor in Memory's mellow wine
That makes me drink the deeper to that old sweetheart of mine.

A face of lily-beauty, with a form of airy grace.
Floats out of my tobacco as the genii from the vase;
And I thrill beneath the glances of a pair of azure eyes
As glowing as the summer and as tender as the skies.

I can see the pink sunbonnet and the little checkered dress
She wore when first I kissed her and she answered the caress

With the written declaration that, "as surely as the vine
Grew round the stump," she loved me, that old sweetheart of mine.

And again I feel the pressure of her slender little hand,
As we used to talk together of the future we had planned
When I should be a poet, and with nothing else to do
But write the tender verses that she set the music to:

When we should live together in a cozy little cot
Hid in a nest of roses, with a fairy garden-spot,
Where the vines were ever fruited, and the weather ever fine,
And the birds were ever singing for that old sweetheart of mine:

When I should be her lover forever and a day,
And she my faithful sweetheart till the golden hair was gray;
And we should be so happy that when either's lips were dumb
They would not smile in Heaven till the other's kiss had come.

But, ah! my dream is broken by a step upon the stair,
And the door is softly opened, and my wife is standing there;
Yet with eagerness and rapture all my visions I resign
To greet the living presence of that old sweetheart of mine.


A' OLD PLAYED-OUT SONG
It's the curiousest thing in creation,
Whenever I hear that old song
"Do They Miss Me at Home," I'm so bothered,
My life seems as short as it's long!
Fer ev'rything 'pears like adzackly
It 'peared in the years past and gone,
When I started out sparkin', at twenty,
And had my first neckercher on!

Though I'm wrinkelder, older and grayer
Right now than my parents was then,
You strike up that song "Do They Miss Me,"
And I'm jest a youngster again!
I'm a-standin' back thare in the furries
A-wishin' fer evening to come,
And a-whisperin' over and over
Them words "Do They Miss Me at Home?"

You see, Marthy Ellen she sung it
The first time I heerd it; and so,
As she was my very first sweetheart,
It reminds me of her, don't you know;
How her face used to look, in the twilight,
As I tuck her to Spellin'; and she
Kep' a-hummin' that song tel I ast her,

Pint-blank, ef she ever missed me!

I can shet my eyes now, as you sing it,
And hear her low answerin' words;
And then the glad chirp of the crickets,
As clear as the twitter of birds;
And the dust in the road is like velvet,
And the ragweed and fennel and grass
Is as sweet as the scent of the lilies
Of Eden of old, as we pass.

"Do They Miss Me at Home?" Sing it lower
And softer and sweet as the breeze
That powdered our path with the snowy
White bloom of the old locus'-trees!
Let the whipperwills he'p you to sing it,
And the echoes 'way over the hill,
Tel the moon boolges out, in a chorus
Of stars, and our voices is still.

But oh! "They's a chord in the music
That's missed when her voice is away!"
Though I listen from midnight tel morning,
And dawn tel the dusk of the day!
And I grope through the dark, lookin' upwards
And on through the heavenly dome,
With my longin' soul singin' and sobbin'
The words "Do They Miss Me at Home?"


### A VERY YOUTHFUL AFFAIR
I'm bin a-visitun 'bout a week
To my little Cousin's at Nameless Creek,
An' I'm got the hives an' a new straw hat,
An' I'm come back home where my beau lives at.


### AN OUT-WORN SAPPHO
How tired I am! I sink down all alone
Here by the wayside of the Present. Lo,
Even as a child I hide my face and moan
A little girl that may no farther go;
The path above me only seems to grow
More rugged, climbing still, and ever briered
With keener thorns of pain than these below;
And O the bleeding feet that falter so
And are so very tired!

Why, I have journeyed from the far-off Lands

Of Babyhood where baby-lilies blew
Their trumpets in mine ears, and filled my hands
With treasures of perfume and honey-dew,
And where the orchard shadows ever drew
Their cool arms round me when my cheeks were fired
With too much joy, and lulled mine eyelids to,
And only let the starshine trickle through
In sprays, when I was tired!

Yet I remember, when the butterfly
Went flickering about me like a flame
That quenched itself in roses suddenly,
How oft I wished that I might blaze the same,
And in some rose-wreath nestle with my name,
While all the world looked on it and admired.
Poor moth! Along my wavering flight toward fame
The winds drive backward, and my wings are lame
And broken, bruised and tired!

I hardly know the path from those old times;
I know at first it was a smoother one
Than this that hurries past me now, and climbs
So high, its far cliffs even hide the sun
And shroud in gloom my journey scarce begun.
I could not do quite all the world required
I could not do quite all I should have done,
And in my eagerness I have outrun
My strength and I am tired....

Just tired! But when of old I had the stay
Of mother-hands, O very sweet indeed
It was to dream that all the weary way
I should but follow where I now must lead
For long ago they left me in my need,
And, groping on alone, I tripped and mired
Among rank grasses where the serpents breed
In knotted coils about the feet of speed.
There first it was I tired.

And yet I staggered on, and bore my load
Right gallantly: The sun, in summer-time,
In lazy belts came slipping down the road
To woo me on, with many a glimmering rhyme
Rained from the golden rim of some fair clime,
That, hovering beyond the clouds, inspired
My failing heart with fancies so sublime
I half forgot my path of dust and grime,
Though I was growing tired.

And there were many voices cheering me:
I listened to sweet praises where the wind

Went laughing o'er my shoulders gleefully
And scattering my love-songs far behind;
Until, at last, I thought the world so kind
So rich in all my yearning soul desired
So generous, so loyally inclined,
I grew to love and trust it.... I was blind
Yea, blind as I was tired!

And yet one hand held me in creature-touch:
And O, how fair it was, how true and strong,
How it did hold my heart up like a crutch,
Till, in my dreams, I joyed to walk along
The toilsome way, contented with a song
'Twas all of earthly things I had acquired,
And 'twas enough, I feigned, or right or wrong,
Since, binding me to man, a mortal thong
It stayed me, growing tired....

Yea, I had e'en resigned me to the strait
Of earthly rulership had bowed my head
Acceptant of the master-mind the great
One lover, lord of all, the perfected
Kiss-comrade of my soul; had stammering said
My prayers to him; all, all that he desired
I rendered sacredly as we were wed.
Nay, nay! 'twas but a myth I worshippéd.
And God of love! how tired!

For, O my friends, to lose the latest grasp
To feel the last hope slipping from its hold
To feel the one fond hand within your clasp
Fall slack, and loosen with a touch so cold
Its pressure may not warm you as of old
Before the light of love had thus expired
To know your tears are worthless, though they rolled
Their torrents out in molten drops of gold.
God's pity! I am tired!

And I must rest. Yet do not say "She died,"
In speaking of me, sleeping here alone.
I kiss the grassy grave I sink beside,
And close mine eyes in slumber all mine own:
Hereafter I shall neither sob nor moan
Nor murmur one complaint; all I desired,
And failed in life to find, will now be known
So let me dream. Good night! And on the stone
Say simply: She was tired.

THE PASSING OF A HEART

O touch me with your hands
For pity's sake!
My brow throbs ever on with such an ache
As only your cool touch may take away;
And so, I pray
You, touch me with your hands!

Touch, touch me with your hands.
Smooth back the hair
You once caressed, and kissed, and called so fair
That I did dream its gold would wear alway,
And lo, to-day
O touch me with your hands!

Just touch me with your hands,
And let them press
My weary eyelids with the old caress,
And lull me till I sleep. Then go your way,
That Death may say:
He touched her with his hands.


"DREAM"
Because her eyes were far too deep
And holy for a laugh to leap
Across the brink where sorrow tried
To drown within the amber tide;
Because the looks, whose ripples kissed
The trembling lids through tender mist,
Were dazzled with a radiant gleam
Because of this I call her "Dream."

Because the roses growing wild
About her features when she smiled
Were ever dewed with tears that fell
With tenderness ineffable;
Because her lips might spill a kiss
That, dripping in a world like this,
Would tincture death's myrrh-bitter stream
To sweetness so I called her "Dream."

Because I could not understand
The magic touches of a hand
That seemed, beneath her strange control,
To smooth the plumage of the soul
And calm it, till, with folded wings,
It half forgot its flutterings,
And, nestled in her palm, did seem
To trill a song that called her "Dream."

Because I saw her, in a sleep
As dark and desolate and deep
And fleeting as the taunting night
That flings a vision of delight
To some lorn martyr as he lies
In slumber ere the day he dies
Because she vanished like a gleam
Of glory, do I call her "Dream."


## HE CALLED HER IN

I

He called her in from me and shut the door.
And she so loved the sunshine and the sky!
She loved them even better yet than I
That ne'er knew dearth of them, my mother dead,
Nature had nursed me in her lap instead:
And I had grown a dark and eerie child
That rarely smiled,
Save when, shut all alone in grasses high,
Looking straight up in God's great lonesome sky
And coaxing Mother to smile back on me.
'Twas lying thus, this fair girl suddenly
Came to me, nestled in the fields beside
A pleasant-seeming home, with doorway wide
The sunshine beating in upon the floor
Like golden rain.
O sweet, sweet face above me, turn again
And leave me! I had cried, but that an ache
Within my throat so gripped it I could make
No sound but a thick sobbing. Cowering so,
I felt her light hand laid
Upon my hair, a touch that ne'er before
Had tamed me thus, all soothed and unafraid
It seemed the touch the children used to know
When Christ was here, so dear it was so dear,
At once I loved her as the leaves love dew
In midmost summer when the days are new.
Barely an hour I knew her, yet a curl
Of silken sunshine did she clip for me
Out of the bright May-morning of her hair,
And bound and gave it to me laughingly,
And caught my hands and called me "Little girl,"
Tiptoeing, as she spoke, to kiss me there!
And I stood dazed and dumb for very stress
Of my great happiness.
She plucked me by the gown, nor saw how mean
The raiment drew me with her everywhere:
Smothered her face in tufts of grasses green:
Put up her dainty hands and peeped between

Her fingers at the blossoms crooned and talked
To them in strange, glad whispers, as we walked,
Said this one was her angel mother this,
Her baby-sister come back, for a kiss,
Clean from the Good-World! smiled and kissed them, then
Closed her soft eyes and kissed them o'er again.
And so did she beguile me so we played,
She was the dazzling Shine I, the dark Shade
And we did mingle like to these, and thus,
Together, made
The perfect summer, pure and glorious.
So blent we, till a harsh voice broke upon
Our happiness. She, startled as a fawn,
Cried, "Oh, 'tis Father!" all the blossoms gone
From out her cheeks as those from out her grasp.
Harsher the voice came: She could only gasp
Affrightedly, "Good-bye! good-bye! good-bye!"
And lo, I stood alone, with that harsh cry
Ringing a new and unknown sense of shame
Through soul and frame,
And, with wet eyes, repeating o'er and o'er,
"He called her in from me and shut the door!"


II

He called her in from me and shut the door!
And I went wandering alone again
So lonely O so very lonely then,
I thought no little sallow star, alone
In all a world of twilight, e'er had known
Such utter loneliness. But that I wore
Above my heart that gleaming tress of hair
To lighten up the night of my despair,
I think I might have groped into my grave
Nor cared to wave
The ferns above it with a breath of prayer.
And how I hungered for the sweet, sweet face
That bent above me in my hiding-place
That day amid the grasses there beside
Her pleasant home! "Her pleasant home!" I sighed,
Remembering; then shut my teeth and feigned
The harsh voice calling me, then clinched my nails
So deeply in my palms, the sharp wounds pained,
And tossed my face toward heaven, as one who pales
In splendid martrydom, with soul serene,
As near to God as high the guillotine.

And I had envied her? Not that O no!
But I had longed for some sweet haven so!
Wherein the tempest-beaten heart might ride
Sometimes at peaceful anchor, and abide

Where those that loved me touched me with their hands,
And looked upon me with glad eyes, and slipped
Smooth fingers o'er my brow, and lulled the strands
Of my wild tresses, as they backward tipped
My yearning face and kissed it satisfied.
Then bitterly I murmured as before,
"He called her in from me and shut the door!"

III

He called her in from me and shut the door!
After long struggling with my pride and pain
A weary while it seemed, in which the more
I held myself from her, the greater fain
Was I to look upon her face again;
At last, at last, half conscious where my feet
Were faring, I stood waist-deep in the sweet
Green grasses there where she
First came to me.
The very blossoms she had plucked that day,
And, at her father's voice, had cast away,
Around me lay,
Still bright and blooming in these eyes of mine;
And as I gathered each one eagerly,
I pressed it to my lips and drank the wine
Her kisses left there for the honey-bee.
Then, after I had laid them with the tress
Of her bright hair with lingering tenderness,
I, turning, crept on to the hedge that bound
Her pleasant-seeming home but all around
Was never sign of her! The windows all
Were blinded; and I heard no rippling fall
Of her glad laugh, nor any harsh voice call;
But clutching to the tangled grasses, caught
A sound as though a strong man bowed his head
And sobbed alone, unloved, uncomforted!
And then straightway before
My tearless eyes, all vividly, was wrought
A vision that is with me evermore:
A little girl that lies asleep, nor hears
Nor heeds not any voice nor fall of tears.
And I sit singing o'er and o'er and o'er,
"God called her in from him and shut the door!"

HER FACE AND BROW
Ah, help me! but her face and brow
Are lovelier than lilies are
Beneath the light of moon and star
That smile as they are smiling now
White lilies in a pallid swoon

Of sweetest white beneath the moon
White lilies, in a flood of bright
Pure lucidness of liquid light
Cascading down some plenilune,
When all the azure overhead
Blooms like a dazzling daisy-bed.
So luminous her face and brow,
The luster of their glory, shed
In memory, even, blinds me now.


HER BEAUTIFUL EYES
O her beautiful eyes! they are blue as the dew
On the violet's bloom when the morning is new,
And the light of their love is the gleam of the sun
O'er the meadows of Spring where the quick shadows run
As the morn shifts the mists and the clouds from the skies
So I stand in the dawn of her beautiful eyes.

And her beautiful eyes are as mid-day to me,
When the lily-bell bends with the weight of the bee,
And the throat of the thrush is a-pulse in the heat,
And the senses are drugged with the subtle and sweet
And delirious breaths of the air's lullabies
So I swoon in the noon of her beautiful eyes.

O her beautiful eyes! they have smitten mine own
As a glory glanced down from the glare of the Throne;
And I reel, and I falter and fall, as afar
Fell the shepherds that looked on the mystical Star,
And yet dazed in the tidings that bade them arise
So I groped through the night of her beautiful eyes.


WHEN SHE COMES HOME
When she comes home again! A thousand ways
I fashion, to myself, the tenderness
Of my glad welcome: I shall tremble yes;
And touch her, as when first in the old days
I touched her girlish hand, nor dared upraise
Mine eyes, such was my faint heart's sweet distress.
Then silence: And the perfume of her dress:
The room will sway a little, and a haze
Cloy eyesight, soulsight, even, for a space:
And tears, yes; and the ache here in the throat,
To know that I so ill deserve the place
Her arms make for me; and the sobbing note
I stay with kisses, ere the tearful face
Again is hidden in the old embrace.

## LET US FORGET

Let us forget. What matters it that we
Once reigned o'er happy realms of long-ago,
And talked of love, and let our voices low,
And ruled for some brief sessions royally?
What if we sung, or laughed, or wept maybe?
It has availed not anything, and so
Let it go by that we may better know
How poor a thing is lost to you and me.
But yesterday I kissed your lips, and yet
Did thrill you not enough to shake the dew
From your drenched lids and missed, with no regret,
Your kiss shot back, with sharp breaths failing you:
And so, to-day, while our worn eyes are wet
With all this waste of tears, let us forget!


## LEONAINIE

Leonainie, Angels named her;
And they took the light
Of the laughing stars and framed her
In a smile of white;
And they made her hair of gloomy
Midnight, and her eyes of bloomy
Moonshine, and they brought her to me
In the solemn night.

In a solemn night of summer,
When my heart of gloom
Blossomed up to greet the comer
Like a rose in bloom;
All forebodings that distressed me
I forgot as Joy caressed me,
(Lying Joy! that caught and pressed me
In the arms of doom!)

Only spake the little lisper
In the Angel-tongue;
Yet I, listening, heard her whisper
"Songs are only sung
Here below that they may grieve you,
Tales but told you to deceive you,
So must Leonainie leave you
While her love is young,"

Then God smiled and it was morning
Matchless and supreme

Heaven's glory seemed adorning
Earth with its esteem:
Every heart but mine seemed gifted
With the voice of prayer, and lifted
Where my Leonainie drifted
From me like a dream.


HER WAITING FACE
In some strange place
Of long-lost lands he finds her waiting face
Comes marveling upon it, unaware,
Set moonwise in the midnight of her hair.


THE OLD YEAR AND THE NEW
I
As one in sorrow looks upon
The dead face of a loyal friend,
By the dim light of New Year's dawn
I saw the Old Year end.

Upon the pallid features lay
The dear old smile, so warm and bright
Ere thus its cheer had died away
In ashes of delight.

The hands that I had learned to love
With strength of passion half divine,
Were folded now, all heedless of
The emptiness of mine.

The eyes that once had shed their bright
Sweet looks like sunshine, now were dull,
And ever lidded from the light
That made them beautiful.

II
The chimes of bells were in the air,
And sounds of mirth in hall and street,
With pealing laughter everywhere
And throb of dancing feet:

The mirth and the convivial din
Of revelers in wanton glee,
With tunes of harp and violin
In tangled harmony.

But with a sense of nameless dread,

I turned me, from the merry face
Of this newcomer, to my dead;
And, kneeling there a space,

I sobbed aloud, all tearfully:
By this dear face so fixed and cold,
O Lord, let not this New Year be
As happy as the old!


THEIR SWEET SORROW
They meet to say farewell: Their way
Of saying this is hard to say.
He holds her hand an instant, wholly
Distressed and she unclasps it slowly.

He bends his gaze evasively
Over the printed page that she
Recurs to, with a new-moon shoulder
Glimpsed from the lace-mists that enfold her.

The clock, beneath its crystal cup,
Discreetly clicks "Quick! Act! Speak up!"
A tension circles both her slender
Wrists and her raised eyes flash in splendor,

Even as he feels his dazzled own.
Then, blindingly, round either thrown,
They feel a stress of arms that ever
Strain tremblingly and "Never! Never!"

Is whispered brokenly, with half
A sob, like a belated laugh,
While cloyingly their blurred kiss closes,
Sweet as the dew's lip to the rose's.


JUDITH
O Her eyes are amber-fine
Dark and deep as wells of wine,
While her smile is like the noon
Splendor of a day of June,
If she sorrow, lo! her face
It is like a flowery space
In bright meadows, overlaid
With light clouds and lulled with shade.
If she laugh, it is the trill
Of the wayward whippoorwill
Over upland pastures, heard

Echoed by the mocking-bird
In dim thickets dense with bloom
And blurred cloyings of perfume.
If she sigh, a zephyr swells
Over odorous asphodels
And wall lilies in lush plots
Of moon-drown'd forget-me-nots.
Then, the soft touch of her hand
Takes all breath to understand
What to liken it thereto!
Never roseleaf rinsed with dew
Might slip soother-suave than slips
Her slow palm, the while her lips
Swoon through mine, with kiss on kiss
Sweet as heated honey is.


HE AND I

Just drifting on together
He and I
As through the balmy weather
Of July
Drift two thistle-tufts imbedded
Each in each by zephyrs wedded
Touring upward, giddy-headed,
For the sky.

And, veering up and onward,
Do we seem
Forever drifting dawnward
In a dream,
Where we meet song-birds that know us,
And the winds their kisses blow us,
While the years flow far below us
Like a stream.

And we are happy, very
He and I
Aye, even glad and merry
Though on high
The heavens are sometimes shrouded
By the midnight storm, and clouded
Till the pallid moon is crowded
From the sky.

My spirit ne'er expresses
Any choice
But to clothe him with caresses
And rejoice;
And as he laughs, it is in

Such a tone the moonbeams glisten
And the stars come out to listen
To his voice.

And so, whate'er the weather,
He and I,
With our lives linked thus together,
Float and fly
As two thistle-tufts imbedded
Each in each by zephyrs wedded
Touring upward, giddy-headed,
For the sky.


THE LOST PATH
Alone they walked, their fingers knit together,
And swaying listlessly as might a swing
Wherein Dan Cupid dangled in the weather
Of some sun-flooded afternoon of Spring.

Within the clover-fields the tickled cricket
Laughed lightly as they loitered down the lane,
And from the covert of the hazel-thicket
The squirrel peeped and laughed at them again.

The bumble-bee that tipped the lily-vases
Along the road-side in the shadows dim,
Went following the blossoms of their faces
As though their sweets must needs be shared with him.

Between the pasture bars the wondering cattle
Stared wistfully, and from their mellow bells
Shook out a welcoming whose dreamy rattle
Fell swooningly away in faint farewells.

And though at last the gloom of night fell o'er them
And folded all the landscape from their eyes,
They only knew the dusky path before them
Was leading safely on to Paradise.


MY BRIDE THAT IS TO BE
O soul of mine, look out and see
My bride, my bride that is to be!
Reach out with mad, impatient hands,
And draw aside futurity
As one might draw a veil aside
And so unveil her where she stands
Madonna-like and glorified

The queen of undiscovered lands
Of love, to where she beckons me
My bride, my bride that is to be.

The shadow of a willow-tree
That wavers on a garden-wall
In summertime may never fall
In attitude as gracefully
As my fair bride that is to be;
Nor ever Autumn's leaves of brown
As lightly flutter to the lawn
As fall her fairy-feet upon
The path of love she loiters down.
O'er drops of dew she walks, and yet
Not one may stain her sandal wet
Aye, she might dance upon the way
Nor crush a single drop to spray,
So airy-like she seems to me,
My bride, my bride that is to be.

I know not if her eyes are light
As summer skies or dark as night,
I only know that they are dim
With mystery: In vain I peer
To make their hidden meaning clear,
While o'er their surface, like a tear
That ripples to the silken brim,
A look of longing seems to swim

All worn and wearylike to me;
And then, as suddenly, my sight
Is blinded with a smile so bright,
Through folded lids I still may see
My bride, my bride that is to be.

Her face is like a night of June
Upon whose brow the crescent-moon
Hangs pendant in a diadem
Of stars, with envy lighting them.
And, like a wild cascade, her hair
Floods neck and shoulder, arm and wrist,
Till only through a gleaming mist
I seem to see a siren there,
With lips of love and melody
And open arms and heaving breast
Wherein I fling myself to rest,
The while my heart cries hopelessly
For my fair bride that is to be...

Nay, foolish heart and blinded eyes!
My bride hath need of no disguise.

But, rather, let her come to me
In such a form as bent above
My pillow when in infancy
I knew not anything but love.
O let her come from out the lands
Of Womanhood, not fairy isles,
And let her come with Woman's hands
And Woman's eyes of tears and smiles,
With Woman's hopefulness and grace
Of patience lighting up her face:
And let her diadem be wrought
Of kindly deed and prayerful thought,
That ever over all distress
May beam the light of cheerfulness.
And let her feet be brave to fare
The labyrinths of doubt and care,
That, following, my own may find
The path to Heaven God designed.
O let her come like this to me
My bride, my bride that is to be.


HOW IT HAPPENED

I got to thinkin' of her, both her parents dead and gone
And all her sisters married off, and none but her and John
A-livin' all alone there in that lonesome sort o' way,
And him a blame' old bachelor, confirm'der ev'ry day!
I'd knowed 'em all from childern, and their daddy from the time
He settled in the neighberhood, and hadn't airy a dime
Er dollar, when he married, fer to start housekeepin' on!
So I got to thinkin' of her, both her parents dead and gone!

I got to thinkin' of her; and a-wundern what she done
That all her sisters kep' a-gittin' married, one by one,
And her without no chances and the best girl of the pack
An old maid, with her hands, you might say, tied behind her back!
And Mother, too, afore she died, she ust to jes' take on,
When none of 'em was left, you know, but Evaline and John,
And jes' declare to goodness 'at the young men must be bline
To not see what a wife they'd git if they got Evaline!

I got to thinkin' of her; in my great affliction she
Was sich a comfert to us, and so kind and neighberly,
She'd come, and leave her housework, fer to he'p out little Jane,
And talk of her own mother 'at she'd never see again
Maybe sometimes cry together, though, fer the most part she
Would have the child so riconciled and happy-like 'at we
Felt lonesomer 'n ever when she'd put her bonnet on
And say she'd railly haf to be a-gittin' back to John!

I got to thinkin' of her, as I say, and more and more
I'd think of her dependence, and the burdens 'at she bore,
Her parents both a-bein' dead, and all her sisters gone
And married off, and her a-livin' there alone with John
You might say jes' a-toilin' and a-slavin' out her life
Fer a man 'at hadn't pride enough to git hisse'f a wife
'Less some one married Evaline and packed her off some day!
So I got to thinkin' of her and it happened that-away.


WHEN MY DREAMS COME TRUE
I
When my dreams come true, when my dreams come true
Shall I lean from out my casement, in the starlight and the dew,
To listen, smile and listen to the tinkle of the strings
Of the sweet guitar my lover's fingers fondle, as he sings?
And the nude moon slowly, slowly shoulders into view,
Shall I vanish from his vision, when my dreams come true?

When my dreams come true, shall the simple gown I wear
Be changed to softest satin, and my maiden-braided hair
Be raveled into flossy mists of rarest, fairest gold,
To be minted into kisses, more than any heart can hold?
Or "the summer of my tresses" shall my lover liken to
"The fervor of his passion" when my dreams come true?

II
When my dreams come true, I shall bide among the sheaves
Of happy harvest meadows; and the grasses and the leaves
Shall lift and lean between me and the splendor of the sun,
Till the moon swoons into twilight, and the gleaners' work is done
Save that yet an arm shall bind me, even as the reapers do
The meanest sheaf of harvest, when my dreams come true.

When my dreams come true! when my dreams come true!
True love in all simplicity is fresh and pure as dew;
The blossom in the blackest mold is kindlier to the eye
Than any lily born of pride that looms against the sky:
And so it is I know my heart will gladly welcome you,
My lowliest of lovers, when my dreams come true.


NOTHIN' TO SAY
Nothin' to say, my daughter! Nothin' at all to say!
Gyrls that's in love, I've noticed, ginerly has their way!
Yer mother did afore you, when her folks objected to me
Yit here I am, and here you air; and yer mother, where is she?

You look lots like yer mother: Purty much same in size;

And about the same complected; and favor about the eyes:
Like her, too, about livin' here, because she couldn't stay:
It'll 'most seem like you was dead like her! But I hain't got nothin' to say!

She left you her little Bible, writ yer name acrost the page
And left her ear bobs fer you, ef ever you come of age.
I've allus kep'em and gyuarded 'em, but ef yer goin' away
Nothin' to say, my daughter! Nothin' at all to say!

You don't rikollect her, I reckon? No; you wasn't a year old then!
And now yer, how old air you? W'y, child, not "twenty!" When?
And yer nex' birthday's in Aprile? and you want to git married that day?
I wisht yer mother was livin'! But I hain't got nothin' to say!

Twenty year! and as good a gyrl as parent ever found!
There's a straw ketched onto yer dress there, I'll bresh it off, turn around.
(Her mother was jes' twenty when us two run away!)
Nothin' to say, my daughter! Nothin' at all to say!


**IKE WALTON'S PRAYER**
I crave, dear Lord,
No boundless hoard
Of gold and gear,
Nor jewels fine,
Nor lands, nor kine,
Nor treasure-heaps of anything.
Let but a little hut be mine
Where at the hearthstone I may hear
The cricket sing,
And have the shine
Of one glad woman's eyes to make,
For my poor sake,
Our simple home a place divine;
Just the wee cot, the cricket's chirr
Love, and the smiling face of her.

I pray not for
Great riches, nor
For vast estates, and castle-halls,
Give me to hear the bare footfalls
Of children o'er
An oaken floor,
New-rinsed with sunshine, or bespread
With but the tiny coverlet
And pillow for the baby's head;
And pray Thou, may
The door stand open and the day
Send ever in a gentle breeze,
With fragrance from the locust-trees,

And drowsy moan of doves, and blur
Of robin-chirps, and drone of bees,

With afterhushes of the stir
Of intermingling sounds, and then
The good-wife and the smile of her
Filling the silences again
The cricket's call,
And the wee cot,
Dear Lord of all,
Deny me not!

I pray not that
Men tremble at
My power of place
And lordly sway,
I only pray for simple grace
To look my neighbor in the face
Full honestly from day to day
Yield me his horny palm to hold,
And I'll not pray
For gold;
The tanned face, garlanded with mirth,
It hath the kingliest smile on earth
The swart brow, diamonded with sweat,
Hath never need of coronet.
And so I reach,
Dear Lord, to Thee,
And do beseech
Thou givest me
The wee cot, and the cricket's chirr,
Love, and the glad sweet face of her.


ILLILEO
Illileo, the moonlight seemed lost across the vales
The stars but strewed the azure as an armor's scattered scales;
The airs of night were quiet as the breath of silken sails;
And all your words were sweeter than the notes of nightingales.

Illileo Legardi, in the garden there alone,
With your figure carved of fervor, as the Psyche carved of stone,
There came to me no murmur of the fountain's undertone
So mystically, musically mellow as your own.

You whispered low, Illileo, so low the leaves were mute,
And the echoes faltered breathless in your voice's vain pursuit;
And there died the distant dalliance of the serenader's lute:
And I held you in my bosom as the husk may hold the fruit.

Illileo, I listened. I believed you. In my bliss,
What were all the worlds above me since I found you thus in this?
Let them reeling reach to win me - even Heaven I would miss,
Grasping earthward! I would cling here, though I clung by just a kiss!

And blossoms should grow odorless and lilies all aghast
And I said the stars should slacken in their paces through the vast,
Ere yet my loyalty should fail enduring to the last.
So vowed I. It is written. It is changeless as the past.

Illileo Legardi, in the shade your palace throws
Like a cowl about the singer at your gilded porticos,
A moan goes with the music that may vex the high repose
Of a heart that fades and crumbles as the crimson of a rose.


THE WIFE-BLESSÉD
I
In youth he wrought, with eyes ablur
Lorn-faced and long of hair
In youth, in youth he painted her
A sister of the air
Could clasp her not, but felt the stir
Of pinions everywhere.

II
She lured his gaze, in braver days,
And tranced him sirenwise;
And he did paint her, through a haze
Of sullen paradise,
With scars of kisses on her face
And embers in her eyes.

III
And now, nor dream nor wild conceit
Though faltering, as before
Through tears he paints her, as is meet,
Tracing the dear face o'er
With lilied patience meek and sweet
As Mother Mary wore.


MY MARY
My Mary, O my Mary!
The simmer-skies are blue;
The dawnin' brings the dazzle,
An' the gloamin' brings the dew?
The mirk o' nicht the glory
O' the moon, an' kindles, too,

The stars that shift aboon the lift.
But nae thing brings me you!

Where is it, O my Mary,
Ye are biding a' the while?
I ha' wended by your window
I ha' waited by the stile,
An' up an' down the river
I ha' won for mony a mile,
Yet never found, adrift or drown'd,
Your lang-belated smile.

Is it forgot, my Mary,
How glad we used to be?
The simmer-time when bonny bloomed
The auld trysting-tree,
How there I carved the name for you,
An' you the name for me;
An' the gloamin' kenned it only
When we kissed sae tenderly.

Speek ance to me, my Mary!
But whisper in my ear
As light as ony sleeper's breath,
An' a' my soul will hear;
My heart shall stap its beating
An' the soughing atmosphere
Be hushed the while I leaning smile
An' listen to you, dear!

My Mary, O my Mary!
The blossoms bring the bees;
The sunshine brings the blossoms,
An' the leaves on a' the trees;
The simmer brings the sunshine
An' the fragrance o' the breeze,
But O wi'out you, Mary,
I care nae thing for these!

We were sae happy, Mary!
O think how ance we said
Wad ane o' us gae fickle,
Or are o' us lie dead,
To feel anither's kisses
We wad feign the auld instead,
And ken the ither's footsteps
In the green grass owerhead.

My Mary, O my Mary!
Are ye daughter o' the air,
That ye vanish aye before me

As I follow everywhere?
Or is it ye are only
But a mortal, wan wi' care?
Syne I search through a' the kirkyird
An' I dinna find ye there!


## HOME AT NIGHT

When chirping crickets fainter cry,
And pale stars blossom in the sky,
And twilight's gloom has dimmed the bloom
And blurred the butterfly:

When locust-blossoms fleck the walk,
And up the tiger-lily stalk
The glow-worm crawls and clings and falls
And glimmers down the garden-walls:

When buzzing things, with double wings
Of crisp and raspish flutterings,
Go whizzing by so very nigh
One thinks of fangs and stings:

O then, within, is stilled the din
Of crib she rocks the baby in,
And heart and gate and latch's weight
Are lifted and the lips of Kate,


## WHEN LIDE MARRIED HIM

When Lide married him, w'y, she had to jes dee-fy
The whole poppilation! But she never bat' an eye!
Her parents begged, and threatened, she must give him up, that he
Wuz jes "a common drunkard!" And he wuz, appearantly.
Swore they'd chase him off the place
Ef he ever showed his face
Long after she'd eloped with him and married him fer shore!
When Lide married him, it wuz "Katy, bar the door!"

When Lide married him. Well! she had to go and be
A hired girl in town somewheres, while he tromped round to see
What he could git that he could do, you might say, jes sawed wood
From door to door! that's what he done 'cause that wuz best he could!
And the strangest thing, i jing!
Wuz, he didn't drink a thing,
But jes got down to bizness, like he someway wanted to,
When Lide married him, like they warned her not to do!

When Lide married him, er, ruther, had ben married

A little up'ards of a year, some feller come and carried
That hired girl away with him, a ruther stylish feller
In a bran-new green spring-wagon, with the wheels striped red and yeller:
And he whispered, as they driv
Tords the country, "Now we'll live!"
And somepin' else she laughed to hear, though both her eyes wuz dim,
'Bout "trustin' Love and Heav'n above, sence Lide married him!"


HER HAIR
The beauty of her hair bewilders me
Pouring adown the brow, its cloven tide
Swirling about the ears on either side
And storming around the neck tumultuously:
Or like the lights of old antiquity
Through mullioned windows, in cathedrals wide,
Spilled moltenly o'er figures deified
In chastest marble, nude of drapery.
And so I love it. Either unconfined;
Or plaited in close braidings manifold;
Or smoothly drawn; or indolently twined
In careless knots whose coilings come unrolled
At any lightest kiss; or by the wind
Whipped out in flossy ravelings of gold.


LAST NIGHT - AND THIS
Last night, how deep the darkness was!
And well I knew its depths, because
I waded it from shore to shore,
Thinking to reach the light no more.

She would not even touch my hand.
The winds rose and the cedars fanned
The moon out, and the stars fled back
In heaven and hid and all was black!

But ah! To-night a summons came,
Signed with a teardrop for a name,
For as I wondering kissed it, lo,
A line beneath it told me so.

And now the moon hangs over me
A disk of dazzling brilliancy,
And every star-tip stabs my sight
With splintered glitterings of light!

A DISCOURAGING MODEL
Just the airiest, fairiest slip of a thing,
With a Gainsborough hat, like a butterfly's wing,
Tilted up at one side with the jauntiest air,
And a knot of red roses sown in under there
Where the shadows are lost in her hair.

Then a cameo face, carven in on a ground
Of that shadowy hair where the roses are wound;
And the gleam of a smile O as fair and as faint
And as sweet as the masters of old used to paint
Round the lips of their favorite saint!

And that lace at her throat and the fluttering hands
Snowing there, with a grace that no art understands
The flakes of their touches, first fluttering at
The bow, then the roses, the hair, and then that
Little tilt of the Gainsborough hat.

What artist on earth, with a model like this,
Holding not on his palette the tint of a kiss,
Nor a pigment to hint of the hue of her hair,
Nor the gold of her smile, O what artist could dare
To expect a result so fair?


SUSPENSE
A woman's figure, on a ground of night
Inlaid with sallow stars that dimly stare
Down in the lonesome eyes, uplifted there
As in vague hope some alien lance of light
Might pierce their woe. The tears that blind her sight
The salt and bitter blood of her despair
Her hands toss back through torrents of her hair
And grip toward God with anguish infinite.
And O the carven mouth, with all its great
Intensity of longing frozen fast
In such a smile as well may designate
The slowly murdered heart, that, to the last
Conceals each newer wound, and back at Fate
Throbs Love's eternal lie "Lo, I can wait!"


THE RIVAL
I so loved once, When Death came by I hid
Away my face,
And all my sweetheart's tresses she undid
To make my hiding-place.

The dread shade passed me thus unheeding; and
I turned me then
To calm my love, kiss down her shielding hand
And comfort her again.

And lo! she answered not: And she did sit
All fixedly,
With her fair face and the sweet smile of it,
In love with Death, not me.


## TOM VAN ARDEN

Tom van Arden, my old friend,
Our warm fellowship is one
Far too old to comprehend
Where its bond was first begun:
Mirage-like before my gaze
Gleams a land of other days,
Where two truant boys, astray,
Dream their lazy lives away.

There's a vision, in the guise
Of Midsummer, where the Past
Like a weary beggar lies
In the shadow Time has cast;
And as blends the bloom of trees
With the drowsy hum of bees,
Fragrant thoughts and murmurs blend,
Tom Van Arden, my old friend.

Tom Van Arden, my old friend,
All the pleasures we have known
Thrill me now as I extend
This old hand and grasp your own
Feeling, in the rude caress,
All affection's tenderness;
Feeling, though the touch be rough,
Our old souls are soft enough.

So we'll make a mellow hour;
Fill your pipe, and taste the wine
Warp your face, if it be sour,
I can spare a smile from mine;
If it sharpen up your wit,
Let me feel the edge of it
I have eager ears to lend,
Tom Van Arden, my old friend.

Tom Van Arden, my old friend,
Are we "lucky dogs," indeed?

Are we all that we pretend
In the jolly life we lead?
Bachelors, we must confess
Boast of "single blessedness"
To the world, but not alone
Man's best sorrow is his own.

And the saddest truth is this,
Life to us has never proved
What we tasted in the kiss
Of the women we have loved:
Vainly we congratulate
Our escape from such a fate
As their lying lips could send,
Tom Van Arden, my old friend!

Tom Van Arden, my old friend,
Hearts, like fruit upon the stem,
Ripen sweetest, I contend,
As the frost falls over them:

Your regard for me to-day
Makes November taste of May,
And through every vein of rhyme
Pours the blood of summertime.

When our souls are cramped with youth
Happiness seems far away
In the future, while, in truth,
We look back on it to-day
Through our tears, nor dare to boast,
"Better to have loved and lost!"
Broken hearts are hard to mend,
Tom Van Arden, my old friend.

Tom Van Arden, my old friend,
I grow prosy, and you tire;
Fill the glasses while I bend
To prod up the failing fire....
You are restless: I presume
There's a dampness in the room.
Much of warmth our nature begs,
With rheumatics in our legs!...

Humph! the legs we used to fling
Limber-jointed in the dance,
When we heard the fiddle ring
Up the curtain of Romance,
And in crowded public halls
Played with hearts like jugglers'-balls.
Feats of mountebanks, depend!

Tom Van Arden, my old friend.

Tom Van Arden, my old friend,
Pardon, then, this theme of mine:
While the fire-light leaps to lend
Higher color to the wine,
I propose a health to those
Who have homes, and home's repose,
Wife and child-love without end!
Tom Van Arden, my old friend.


## TO HEAR HER SING

To hear her sing, to hear her sing
It is to hear the birds of Spring
In dewy groves on blooming sprays
Pour out their blithest roundelays.

It is to hear the robin trill
At morning, or the whippoorwill
At dusk, when stars are blossoming
To hear her sing, to hear her sing!

To hear her sing, it is to hear
The laugh of childhood ringing clear
In woody path or grassy lane
Our feet may never fare again.

Faint, far away as Memory dwells,
It is to hear the village bells
At twilight, as the truant hears
Them, hastening home, with smiles and tears.

Such joy it is to hear her sing,
We fall in love with everything
The simple things of every day
Grow lovelier than words can say.

The idle brooks that purl across
The gleaming pebbles and the moss,
We love no less than classic streams
The Rhines and Arnos of our dreams.

To hear her sing, with folded eyes,
It is, beneath Venetian skies,
To hear the gondoliers' refrain,
Or troubadours of sunny Spain.

To hear the bulbul's voice that shook
The throat that trilled for Lalla Rookh:

What wonder we in homage bring
Our hearts to her, to hear her sing!


A VARIATION
I am tired of this!
Nothing else but loving!
Nothing else but kiss and kiss,
Coo, and turtle-doving!
Can't you change the order some?
Hate me just a little, come!

Lay aside your "dears,"
"Darlings", "kings" and "princes!"
Call me knave, and dry your tears
Nothing in me winces,
Call me something low and base
Something that will suit the case!

Wish I had your eyes
And their drooping lashes!
I would dry their teary lies
Up with lightning-flashes
Make your sobbing lips unsheathe
All the glitter of your teeth!

Can't you lift one word
With some pang of laughter
Louder than the drowsy bird
Crooning 'neath the rafter?
Just one bitter word, to shriek
Madly at me as I speak!

How I hate the fair
Beauty of your forehead!

How I hate your fragrant hair!
How I hate the torrid
Touches of your splendid lips,
And the kiss that drips and drips!

Ah, you pale at last!
And your face is lifted
Like a white sail to the blast,
And your hands are shifted
Into fists: and, towering thus,
You are simply glorious!

Now before me looms
Something more than human;

Something more than beauty blooms
In the wrath of Woman
Something to bow down before
Reverently and adore.


### WHERE SHALL WE LAND?
"Where shall we land you, sweet?" Swinburne.

All listlessly we float
Out seaward in the boat
That beareth Love.
Our sails of purest snow
Bend to the blue below
And to the blue above.
Where shall be land?

We drift upon a tide
Shoreless on every side,
Save where the eye
Of Fancy sweeps far lands
Shelved slopingly with sands
Of gold and porphyry.
Where shall we land?

The fairy isles we see,
Loom up so mistily
So vaguely fair,
We do not care to break
Fresh bubbles in our wake
To bend our course for there.
Where shall we land?

The warm winds of the deep
Have lulled our sails to sleep,
And so we glide
Careless of wave or wind,
Or change of any kind,
Or turn of any tide.
Where shall we land?

We droop our dreamy eyes
Where our reflection lies
Steeped in the sea,
And, in an endless fit
Of languor, smile on it
And its sweet mimicry.
Where shall we land?

"Where shall we land?" God's grace!

I know not any place
So fair as this
Swung here between the blue
Of sea and sky, with you
To ask me, with a kiss,
"Where shall we land?"


## THE TOUCHES OF HER HANDS
The touches of her hands are like the fall
Of velvet snowflakes; like the touch of down
The peach just brushes 'gainst the garden wall;
The flossy fondling of the thistle-wisp
Caught in the crinkle of a leaf of brown
The blighting frost hath turned from green to crisp.

Soft as the falling of the dusk at night,
The touches of her hands, and the delight
The touches of her hands!
The touches of her hands are like the dew
That falls so softly down no one e'er knew
The touch thereof save lovers like to one
Astray in lights where ranged Endymion.

O rarely soft, the touches of her hands,
As drowsy zephyrs in enchanted lands;
Or pulse of dying fay; or fairy sighs;
Or in between the midnight and the dawn,
When long unrest and tears and fears are gone
Sleep, smoothing down the lids of weary eyes.


## FARMER WHIPPLE - BACHELOR
It's a mystery to see me, a man o' fifty-four,
Who's lived a cross old bachelor fer thirty year and more
A-lookin' glad and smilin'! And they's none o' you can say
That you can guess the reason why I feel so good to-day!

I must tell you all about it! But I'll have to deviate
A little in beginning, so's to set the matter straight
As to how it comes to happen that I never took a wife
Kind o' "crawfish" from the Present to the Springtime of my life!

I was brought up in the country: Of a family of five
Three brothers and a sister, I'm the only one alive,
Fer they all died little babies; and 'twas one o' Mother's ways,
You know, to want a daughter; so she took a girl to raise.

The sweetest little thing she was, with rosy cheeks, and fat

We was little chunks o' shavers then about as high as that!
But someway we sort o' suited-like! and Mother she'd declare
She never laid her eyes on a more lovin' pair

Than we was! So we growed up side by side fer thirteen year',
And every hour of it she growed to me more dear!
W'y, even Father's dyin', as he did, I do believe
Warn't more affectin' to me than it was to see her grieve!

I was then a lad o' twenty; and I felt a flash o' pride
In thinkin' all depended on me now to pervide
Fer Mother and fer Mary; and I went about the place
With sleeves rolled up and working with a mighty smilin' face.

Fer sompin' else was workin'! but not a word I said
Of a certain sort o' notion that was runnin' through my head,
"Someday I'd mayby marry, and a brother's love was one
Thing, a lover's was another!" was the way the notion run!

I remember one't in harvest, when the "cradle-in'" was done
When the harvest of my summers mounted up to twenty-one
I was ridin' home with Mary at the closin' o' the day
A-chawin' straws and thinkin', in a lover's lazy way!

And Mary's cheeks was burin' like the sunset down the lane:
I noticed she was thinkin', too, and ast her to explain.
Well, when she turned and kissed me, with her arms around me, law!
I'd a bigger load o' heaven than I had a load o' straw!

I don't p'tend to learnin', but I'll tell you what's a fact,
They's a mighty truthful sayin' somers in a' almanack
Er somers - 'bout "puore happiness" - perhaps some folks'll laugh
At the idy, "only lastin' jest two seconds and a half."

But it's jest as true as preachin'! fer that was a sister's kiss,
And a sister's lovin' confidence a-tellin' to me this:
"She was happy, bein' promised to the son o' farmer Brown."
And my feelin's struck a pardnership with sunset and went down!

I don't know how I acted, I don't know what I said,
Fer my heart seemed jest a-turnin' to an ice-cold lump o' lead;
And the hosses kindo' glimmered before me in the road.
And the lines fell from my fingers and that was all I knowed

Fer well, I don't know how long. They's a dim rememberence
Of a sound o' snortin' hosses, and a stake-and-ridered fence
A-whizzin' past, and wheat-sheaves a-dancin' in the air,
And Mary screamin' "Murder!" and a-runnin' up to where

I was layin' by the road-side, and the wagon upside down
A-leanin' on the gate-post, with the wheels a whirlin' round!

And I tried to raise and meet her, but I couldn't, with a vague
Sorto' notion comin' to me that I had a broken leg.

Well, the women nussed me through it; but many a time I'd sigh
As I'd keep a-gittin' better instid o' goin' to die,
And wonder what was left me worth livin' fer below,
When the girl I loved was married to another, don't you know!

And my thoughts was as rebellious as the folks was good and kind
When Brown and Mary married. Railly must a-been my mind
Was kindo' out o' kilter! fer I hated Brown, you see,
Worse'n pizen and the feller whittled crutches out fer me

And done a thousand little ac's o' kindness and respect
And me a-wishin' all the time that I could break his neck!
My relief was like a mourner's when the funeral is done
When they moved to Illinois in the Fall o' Forty-one.

Then I went to work in airnest, I had nothin' much in view
But to drowned out rickollections and it kep' me busy, too!
But I slowly thrived and prospered, tel Mother used to say
She expected yit to see me a wealthy man some day.

Then I'd think how little money was, compared to happiness
And who'd be left to use it when I died I couldn't guess!
But I've still kep' speculatin' and a-gainin' year by year,
Tel I'm payin' half the taxes in the county, mighty near!

Well! A year ago er better, a letter comes to hand
Astin' how I'd like to dicker fer some Illinois land
"The feller that had owned it," it went ahead to state,
"Had jest deceased, insolvent, leavin' chance to speculate,"

And then it closed by sayin' that I'd "better come and see."
I'd never been West, anyhow, a most too wild fer me
I'd allus had a notion; but a lawyer here in town
Said I'd find myself mistakened when I come to look around.

So I bids good-bye to Mother, and I jumps aboard the train,
A-thinkin' what I'd bring her when I come back home again
And ef she'd had an idy what the present was to be,
I think it's more'n likely she'd a-went along with me!

Cars is awful tejus ridin', fer all they go so fast!
But finally they called out my stoppin'-place at last;
And that night, at the tavern, I dreamp' I was a train
O' cars, and skeered at sompin', runnin' down a country lane!

Well, in the mornin' airly after huntin' up the man
The lawyer who was wantin' to swap the piece o' land
We started fer the country; and I ast the history

Of the farm, its former owner and so-forth, etcetery!

And well it was interestin' I su'prised him, I suppose,
By the loud and frequent manner in which I blowed my nose!
But his surprise was greater, and it made him wonder more,
When I kissed and hugged the widder when she met us at the door!

It was Mary: They's a feelin' a-hidin' down in here
Of course I can't explain it, ner ever make it clear.
It was with us in that meetin', I don't want you to fergit!
And it makes me kind o' nervous when I think about it yit!

I bought that farm, and deeded it, afore I left the town,
With "title clear to mansions in the skies," to Mary Brown!
And fu'thermore, I took her and the childern, fer, you see,
They'd never seed their Grandma and I fetched 'em home with me.

So now you've got an idy why a man o' fifty-four,
Who's lived a cross old bachelor fer thirty year' and more,
Is a-lookin' glad and smilin'! And I've jest come into town
To git a pair o' license fer to marry Mary Brown.


THE ROSE
It tossed its head at the wooing breeze;
And the sun, like a bashful swain,
Beamed on it through the waving trees
With a passion all in vain,
For my rose laughed in a crimson glee,
And hid in the leaves in wait for me.

The honey-bee came there to sing
His love through the languid hours,
And vaunt of his hives, as a proud old king
Might boast of his palace-towers:
But my rose bowed in a mockery,
And hid in the leaves in wait for me.

The humming-bird, like a courtier gay,
Dipped down with a dalliant song,
And twanged his wings through the roundelay
Of love the whole day long:
Yet my rose returned from his minstrelsy
And hid in the leaves in wait for me.

The firefly came in the twilight dim
My red, red rose to woo
Till quenched was the flame of love in him
And the light of his lantern too,
As my rose wept with dewdrops three

And hid in the leaves in wait for me.

And I said: I will cull my own sweet rose
Some day I will claim as mine
The priceless worth of the flower that knows
No change, but a bloom divine
The bloom of a fadeless constancy
That hides in the leaves in wait for me!

But time passed by in a strange disguise,
And I marked it not, but lay
In a lazy dream, with drowsy eyes,
Till the summer slipped away,
And a chill wind sang in a minor key:
"Where is the rose that waits for thee?"

I dream to-day, o'er a purple stain
Of bloom on a withered stalk,
Pelted down by the autumn rain
In the dust of the garden-walk,
That an Angel-rose in the world to be
Will hide in the leaves in wait for me.


WHEN AGE COMES ON
When Age comes on!
The deepening dusk is where the dawn
Once glittered splendid, and the dew
In honey-drips, from red rose-lips
Was kissed away by me and you.
And now across the frosty lawn
Black foot-prints trail, and Age comes on
And Age comes on!
And biting wild-winds whistle through
Our tattered hopes and Age comes on!

When Age comes on!
O tide of raptures, long withdrawn,
Flow back in summer-floods, and fling
Here at our feet our childhood sweet,
And all the songs we used to sing!...
Old loves, old friends all dead and gone
Our old faith lost and Age comes on
And Age comes on!
Poor hearts! have we not anything
But longings left when Age comes on!


HAS SHE FORGOTTEN?

I

Has she forgotten? On this very May
We were to meet here, with the birds and bees,
As on that Sabbath, underneath the trees
We strayed among the tombs, and stripped away
The vines from these old granites, cold and gray
And yet indeed not grim enough were they
To stay our kisses, smiles and ecstasies,
Or closer voice-lost vows and rhapsodies.
Has she forgotten, that the May has won
Its promise? that the bird-songs from the tree
Are sprayed above the grasses as the sun
Might jar the dazzling dew down showeringly?
Has she forgotten life, love, everyone
Has she forgotten me, forgotten me?

II

Low, low down in the violets I press
My lips and whisper to her. Does she hear,
And yet hold silence, though I call her dear,
Just as of old, save for the tearfulness
Of the clenched eyes, and the soul's vast distress?
Has she forgotten thus the old caress
That made our breath a quickened atmosphere
That failed nigh unto swooning with the sheer
Delight? Mine arms clutch now this earthen heap
Sodden with tears that flow on ceaselessly
As autumn rains the long, long, long nights weep
In memory of days that used to be,
Has she forgotten these? And in her sleep,
Has she forgotten me, forgotten me?

III

To-night, against my pillow, with shut eyes,
I mean to weld our faces, through the dense
Incalculable darkness make pretense
That she has risen from her reveries
To mate her dreams with mine in marriages
Of mellow palms, smooth faces, and tense ease
Of every longing nerve of indolence,
Lift from the grave her quiet lips, and stun
My senses with her kisses, drawl the glee
Of her glad mouth, full blithe and tenderly,
Across mine own, forgetful if is done
The old love's awful dawn-time when said we,
"To-day is ours!"... Ah, Heaven! can it be
She has forgotten me, forgotten me!


BLOOMS OF MAY

But yesterday!...
O blooms of May,
And summer roses. Where-away?
O stars above,
And lips of love
And all the honeyed sweets thereof!

O lad and lass
And orchard-pass
And briered lane, and daisied grass!
O gleam and gloom,
And woodland bloom,
And breezy breaths of all perfume!

No more for me
Or mine shall be
Thy raptures, save in memory,
No more, no more
Till through the Door
Of Glory gleam the days of yore.


### THE SERMON OF THE ROSE
Wilful we are in our infirmity
Of childish questioning and discontent.
Whate'er befalls us is divinely meant
Thou Truth the clearer for thy mystery!
Make us to meet what is or is to be
With fervid welcome, knowing it is sent
To serve us in some way full excellent,
Though we discern it all belatedly.
The rose buds, and the rose blooms and the rose
Bows in the dews, and in its fulness, lo,
Is in the lover's hand, then on the breast
Of her he loves, and there dies. And who knows
Which fate of all a rose may undergo
Is fairest, dearest, sweetest, loveliest?

Nay, we are children: we will not mature.
A blessed gift must seem a theft; and tears
Must storm our eyes when but a joy appears
In drear disguise of sorrow; and how poor
We seem when we are richest, most secure
Against all poverty the lifelong years
We yet must waste in childish doubts and fears
That, in despite of reason, still endure!
Alas! the sermon of the rose we will
Not wisely ponder; nor the sobs of grief
Lulled into sighs of rapture; nor the cry
Of fierce defiance that again is still.

Be patient, patient with our frail belief,
And stay it yet a little ere we die.

O opulent life of ours, though dispossessed
Of treasure after treasure! Youth most fair
Went first, but left its priceless coil of hair
Moaned over sleepless nights, kissed and caressed
Through drip and blur of tears the tenderest.
And next went Love, the ripe rose glowing there
Her very sister!... It is here; but where
Is she, of all the world the first and best?
And yet how sweet the sweet earth after rain
How sweet the sunlight on the garden wall
Across the roses and how sweetly flows
The limpid yodel of the brook again!
And yet, and yet how sweeter after all,
The smouldering sweetness of a dead red rose!


## Songs of Home

### WE MUST GET HOME

We must get home! How could we stray like this?
So far from home, we know not where it is,
Only in some fair, apple-blossomy place
Of children's faces and the mother's face
We dimly dream it, till the vision clears
Even in the eyes of fancy, glad with tears.

We must get home, for we have been away
So long, it seems forever and a day!
And O so very homesick we have grown,
The laughter of the world is like a moan
In our tired hearing, and its song as vain,
We must get home, we must get home again!

We must get home! With heart and soul we yearn
To find the long-lost pathway, and return!...
The child's shout lifted from the questing band
Of old folk, faring weary, hand in hand,
But faces brightening, as if clouds at last
Were showering sunshine on us as we passed.

We must get home: It hurts so staying here,
Where fond hearts must be wept out tear by tear,
And where to wear wet lashes means, at best,
When most our lack, the least our hope of rest
When most our need of joy, the more our pain
We must get home, we must get home again!

We must get home, home to the simple things
The morning-glories twirling up the strings
And bugling color, as they blared in blue
And-white o'er garden-gates we scampered through;
The long grape-arbor, with its under-shade
Blue as the green and purple overlaid.

We must get home: All is so quiet there:
The touch of loving hands on brow and hair
Dim rooms, wherein the sunshine is made mild
The lost love of the mother and the child
Restored in restful lullabies of rain,
We must get home, we must get home again!

The rows of sweetcorn and the China beans
Beyond the lettuce-beds where, towering, leans
The giant sunflower in barbaric pride
Guarding the barn-door and the lane outside;
The honeysuckles, midst the hollyhocks,
That clamber almost to the martin-box.

We must get home, where, as we nod and drowse,
Time humors us and tiptoes through the house,
And loves us best when sleeping baby-wise,
With dreams, not tear-drops, brimming our clenched eyes,
Pure dreams that know nor taint nor earthly stain
We must get home, we must get home again!

We must get home! The willow-whistle's call
Trills crisp and liquid as the waterfall
Mocking the trillers in the cherry-trees
And making discord of such rhymes as these,
That know nor lilt nor cadence but the birds
First warbled, then all poets afterwards.

We must get home; and, unremembering there
All gain of all ambition otherwhere,
Rest from the feverish victory, and the crown
Of conquest whose waste glory weighs us down.
Fame's fairest gifts we toss back with disdain
We must get home, we must get home again!

We must get home again, we must, we must!
(Our rainy faces pelted in the dust)
Creep back from the vain quest through endless strife
To find not anywhere in all of life
A happier happiness than blest us then ...
We must get home, we must get home again!

## JUST TO BE GOOD

Just to be good
This is enough, enough!
O we who find sin's billows wild and rough,
Do we not feel how more than any gold
Would be the blameless life we led of old
While yet our lips knew but a mother's kiss?
Ah! though we miss
All else but this,
To be good is enough!

It is enough
Enough, just to be good!
To lift our hearts where they are understood;
To let the thirst for worldly power and place
Go unappeased; to smile back in God's face
With the glad lips our mothers used to kiss.
Ah! though we miss
All else but this,
To be good is enough!


## MY FRIEND

"He is my friend," I said,
"Be patient!" Overhead
The skies were drear and dim;
And lo! the thought of him
Smiled on my heart and then
The sun shone out again!

"He is my friend!" The words
Brought summer and the birds;
And all my winter-time
Thawed into running rhyme
And rippled into song,
Warm, tender, brave and strong.

And so it sings to-day.
So may it sing alway!
Though waving grasses grow
Between, and lilies blow
Their trills of perfume clear
As laughter to the ear,
Let each mute measure end
With "Still he is thy friend."


## THINKIN' BACK

I've ben thinkin' back, of late,
S'prisin'! And I'm here to state
I'm suspicious it's a sign
Of age, maybe, or decline
Of my faculties, and yit
I'm not feelin' old a bit
Any more than sixty-four
Ain't no young man any more!

Thinkin' back's a thing 'at grows
On a feller, I suppose
Older 'at he gits, i jack,
More he keeps a-thinkin' back!
Old as old men git to be,
Er as middle-aged as me,
Folks'll find us, eye and mind
Fixed on what we've left behind
Rehabilitatin'-like
Them old times we used to hike
Out barefooted fer the crick,
'Long 'bout Aprile first to pick
Out some "warmest" place to go
In a-swimmin', Ooh! my-oh!
Wonder now we hadn't died!
Grate horseradish on my hide
Jes' a-thinkin' how cold then
That-'ere worter must 'a' ben!

Thinkin' back. W'y, goodness me!
I kin call their names and see
Every little tad I played
With, er fought, er was afraid
Of, and so made him the best
Friend I had of all the rest!

Thinkin' back, I even hear
Them a-callin', high and clear,
Up the crick-banks, where they seem
Still hid in there like a dream
And me still a-pantin' on
The green pathway they have gone!
Still they hide, by bend er ford
Still they hide but, thank the Lord,
(Thinkin' back, as I have said),
I hear laughin' on ahead!


**NOT ALWAYS GLAD WHEN WE SMILE**
We are not always glad when we smile:
Though we wear a fair face and are gay,

And the world we deceive
May not ever believe
We could laugh in a happier way.
Yet, down in the deeps of the soul,
Ofttimes, with our faces aglow,
There's an ache and a moan
That we know of alone,
And as only the hopeless may know.

We are not always glad when we smile,
For the heart, in a tempest of pain,
May live in the guise
Of a smile in the eyes
As a rainbow may live in the rain;
And the stormiest night of our woe
May hang out a radiant star
Whose light in the sky
Of despair is a lie
As black as the thunder-clouds are.

We are not always glad when we smile!
But the conscience is quick to record,
All the sorrow and sin
We are hiding within
Is plain in the sight of the Lord:
And ever, O ever, till pride
And evasion shall cease to defile
The sacred recess
Of the soul, we confess
We are not always glad when we smile.


## HIS ROOM

"I'm home again, my dear old Room,
I'm home again, and happy, too,
As, peering through the brightening gloom,
I find myself alone with you:
Though brief my stay, nor far away,
I missed you, missed you night and day
As wildly yearned for you as now.
Old Room, how are you, anyhow?

"My easy chair, with open arms,
Awaits me just within the door;
The littered carpet's woven charms
Have never seemed so bright before,
The old rosettes and mignonettes
And ivy-leaves and violets,
Look up as pure and fresh of hue
As though baptized in morning dew.

"Old Room, to me your homely walls
Fold round me like the arms of love,
And over all my being falls
A blessing pure as from above
Even as a nestling child caressed
And lulled upon a loving breast,
With folded eyes, too glad to weep
And yet too sad for dreams or sleep.

"You've been so kind to me, old Room
So patient in your tender care,
My drooping heart in fullest bloom
Has blossomed for you unaware;
And who but you had cared to woo
A heart so dark, and heavy, too,
As in the past you lifted mine
From out the shadow to the shine?

"For I was but a wayward boy
When first you gladly welcomed me
And taught me work was truer joy
Than rioting incessantly:
And thus the din that stormed within
The old guitar and violin
Has fallen in a fainter tone
And sweeter, for your sake alone.

"Though in my absence I have stood
In festal halls a favored guest,
I missed, in this old quietude,
My worthy work and worthy rest
By this I know that long ago
You loved me first, and told me so
In art's mute eloquence of speech
The voice of praise may never reach.

"For lips and eyes in truth's disguise
Confuse the faces of my friends,
Till old affection's fondest ties
I find unraveling at the ends;
But as I turn to you, and learn
To meet my griefs with less concern,
Your love seems all I have to keep
Me smiling lest I needs must weep.

"Yet I am happy, and would fain
Forget the world and all its woes;
So set me to my tasks again,
Old Room, and lull me to repose:
And as we glide adown the tide

Of dreams, forever side by side,
I'll hold your hands as lovers do
Their sweethearts' and talk love to you."


## THE PLAINT HUMAN

Season of snows, and season of flowers,
Seasons of loss and gain!
Since grief and joy must alike be ours,
Why do we still complain?

Ever our failing, from sun to sun,
O my intolerant brother
We want just a little too little of one,
And much too much of the other.


## THE QUEST

I am looking for Love. Has he passed this way,
With eyes as blue as the skies of May,
And a face as fair as the summer dawn?
You answer back, but I wander on,
For you say: "Oh, yes; but his eyes were gray,
And his face as dim as a rainy day."

Good friends, I query, I search for Love;
His eyes are as blue as the skies above,
And his smile as bright as the midst of May
When the truce-bird pipes: Has he passed this way?
And one says: "Ay; but his face, alack!
Frowned as he passed, and his eyes were black."

O who will tell me of Love? I cry!
His eyes are as blue as the mid-May sky,
And his face as bright as the morning sun;
And you answer and mock me, every one,
That his eyes were dark, and his face was wan,
And he passed you frowning and wandered on.

But stout of heart will I onward fare,
Knowing my Love is beyond, somewhere,
The Love I seek, with the eyes of blue,
And the bright, sweet smile unknown of you;
And on from the hour his trail is found
I shall sing sonnets the whole year round.


## THE MULBERRY TREE

It's many's the scenes which is dear to my mind
As I think of my childhood so long left behind;
The home of my birth, with it's old puncheon-floor,
And the bright morning-glories that growed round the door;
The warped clab-board roof whare the rain it run off
Into streams of sweet dreams as I laid in the loft,
Countin' all of the joys that was dearest to me,
And a-thinkin' the most of the mulberry tree.

And to-day as I dream, with both eyes wide-awake,
I can see the old tree, and its limbs as they shake,
And the long purple berries that rained on the ground
Whare the pastur' was bald whare we trommpt it around.
And again, peekin' up through the thick leafy shade,
I can see the glad smiles of the friends when I strayed
With my little bare feet from my own mother's knee
To foller them off to the mulberry tree.

Leanin' up in the forks, I can see the old rail,
And the boy climbin' up it, claw, tooth, and toe-nail,
And in fancy can hear, as he spits on his hands,
The ring of his laugh and the rip of his pants.
But that rail led to glory, as certin and shore
As I'll never climb thare by that rout' any more
What was all the green lauruls of Fame unto me,
With my brows in the boughs of the mulberry tree!

Then it's who can fergit the old mulberry tree
That he knowed in the days when his thoughts was as free
As the flutterin' wings of the birds that flew out
Of the tall wavin' tops as the boys come about?
O, a crowd of my memories, laughin' and gay,
Is a-climbin' the fence of that pastur' to-day,
And, a-pantin' with joy, as us boys ust to be,
They go racin' acrost fer the mulberry tree.


FOR YOU

For you, I could forget the gay
Delirium of merriment,
And let my laughter die away
In endless silence of content.
I could forget, for your dear sake,
The utter emptiness and ache
Of every loss I ever knew.
What could I not forget for you?

I could forget the just deserts
Of mine own sins, and so erase
The tear that burns, the smile that hurts,

And all that mars or masks my face.
For your fair sake I could forget
The bonds of life that chafe and fret,
Nor care if death were false or true.
What could I not forget for you?

What could I not forget? Ah me!
One thing, I know, would still abide
Forever in my memory,
Though all of love were lost beside
I yet would feel how first the wine
Of your sweet lips made fools of mine
Until they sung, all drunken through
"What could I not forget for you?"


A FEEL IN THE CHRIS'MAS-AIR
They's a kind o' feel in the air, to me.
When the Chris'mas-times sets in.
That's about as much of a mystery
As ever I've run ag'in!
Fer instunce, now, whilse I gain in weight
And gineral health, I swear
They's a goneness somers I can't quite state
A kind o' feel in the air.

They's a feel in the Chris'mas-air goes right
To the spot where a man lives at!
It gives a feller a' appetite
They ain't no doubt about that!
And yit they's somepin' I don't know what
That follers me, here and there,
And ha'nts and worries and spares me not
A kind o' feel in the air!

They's a feel, as I say, in the air that's jest
As blame-don sad as sweet!
In the same ra-sho as I feel the best
And am spryest on my feet,
They's allus a kind o' sort of a' ache
That I can't lo-cate no-where;
But it comes with Chris'mas, and no mistake!
A kind o' feel in the air.

Is it the racket the childern raise?
W'y, no! God bless 'em! no!
Is it the eyes and the cheeks ablaze
Like my own wuz, long ago?
Is it the bleat o' the whistle and beat
O' the little toy-drum and blare

O' the horn? No! no! it is jest the sweet
The sad-sweet feel in the air.


AS CREATED

There's a space for good to bloom in
Every heart of man or woman,
And however wild or human,
Or however brimmed with gall,
Never heart may beat without it;
And the darkest heart to doubt it
Has something good about it
After all.


WHERE-AWAY

O the Lands of Where-Away!
Tell us, tell us, where are they?
Through the darkness and the dawn
We have journeyed on and on
From the cradle to the cross
From possession unto loss.
Seeking still, from day to day,
For the Lands of Where-Away.

When our baby-feet were first
Planted where the daisies burst,
And the greenest grasses grew
In the fields we wandered through,
On, with childish discontent,
Ever on and on we went,
Hoping still to pass, some day,
O'er the verge of Where-Away.

Roses laid their velvet lips
On our own, with fragrant sips;
But their kisses held us not,
All their sweetness we forgot;
Though the brambles in our track
Plucked at us to hold us back
"Just ahead," we used to say,
"Lie the Lands of Where-Away."

Children at the pasture-bars,
Through the dusk, like glimmering stars,
Waved their hands that we should bide
With them over eventide;
Down the dark their voices failed
Falteringly, as they hailed,

And died into yesterday
Night ahead and – Where - Away?

Twining arms about us thrown
Warm caresses, all our own,
Can but stay us for a spell
Love hath little new to tell
To the soul in need supreme,
Aching ever with the dream
Of the endless bliss it may
Find in Lands of Where-Away!


### DREAMER, SAY

Dreamer, say, will you dream for me
A wild sweet dream of a foreign land,
Whose border sips of a foaming sea
With lips of coral and silver sand;
Where warm winds loll on the shady deeps,
Or lave themselves in the tearful mist
The great wild wave of the breaker weeps
O'er crags of opal and amethyst?

Dreamer, say, will you dream a dream
Of tropic shades in the lands of shine,
Where the lily leans o'er an amber stream
That flows like a rill of wasted wine,
Where the palm-trees, lifting their shields of green,
Parry the shafts of the Indian sun
Whose splintering vengeance falls between
The reeds below where the waters run?

Dreamer, say, will you dream of love
That lives in a land of sweet perfume,
Where the stars drip down from the skies above
In molten spatters of bud and bloom?
Where never the weary eyes are wet,
And never a sob in the balmy air,
And only the laugh of the paroquette
Breaks the sleep of the silence there?


### OUR OWN

They walk here with us, hand-in-hand;
We gossip, knee-by-knee;
They tell us all that they have planned
Of all their joys to be,
And, laughing, leave us: And, to-day,
All desolate we cry

Across wide waves of voiceless graves
Good-by! Good-by! Good-by!


## THE OLD TRUNDLE-BED

O the old trundle-bed where I slept when a boy!
What canopied king might not covet the joy?
The glory and peace of that slumber of mine,
Like a long, gracious rest in the bosom divine:
The quaint, homely couch, hidden close from the light,
But daintily drawn from its hiding at night.
O a nest of delight, from the foot to the head,
Was the queer little, clear little, old trundle-bed!

O the old trundle-bed, where I wondering saw
The stars through the window, and listened with awe
To the sigh of the winds as they tremblingly crept
Through the trees where the robin so restlessly slept:
Where I heard the low, murmurous chirp of the wren,
And the katydid listlessly chirrup again,
Till my fancies grew faint and were drowsily led
Through the maze of the dreams of the old trundle bed.

O the old trundle-bed! O the old trundle-bed!
With its plump little pillow, and old-fashioned spread;
Its snowy-white sheets, and the blankets above,
Smoothed down and tucked round with the touches of love;
The voice of my mother to lull me to sleep
With the old fairy-stories my memories keep
Still fresh as the lilies that bloom o'er the head
Once bowed o'er my own in the old trundle-bed.


## WHO BIDES HIS TIME

Who bides his time, and day by day
Faces defeat full patiently,
And lifts a mirthful roundelay,
However poor his fortunes be,
He will not fail in any qualm
Of poverty the paltry clime
It will grow golden in his palm,
Who bides his time.

Who bides his time he tastes the sweet
Of honey in the saltest tear;
And though he fares with slowest feet,
Joy runs to meet him, drawing near;
The birds are heralds of his cause;
And, like a never-ending rhyme,

The roadsides bloom in his applause,
Who bides his time.

Who bides his time, and fevers not
In the hot race that none achieves,
Shall wear cool-wreathen laurel, wrought
With crimson berries in the leaves;
And he shall reign a goodly king,
And sway his hand o'er every clime,
With peace writ on his signet-ring,
Who bides his time.


NATURAL PERVERSITIES
I am not prone to moralize
In scientific doubt
On certain facts that Nature tries
To puzzle us about,
For I am no philosopher
Of wise elucidation,
But speak of things as they occur,
From simple observation.

I notice little things to wit:
I never missed a train
Because I didn't run for it;
I never knew it rain
That my umbrella wasn't lent,
Or, when in my possession,
The sun but wore, to all intent,
A jocular expression.

I never knew a creditor
To dun me for a debt
But I was "cramped" or "busted;" or
I never knew one yet,
When I had plenty in my purse,
To make the least invasion,
As I, accordingly perverse,
Have courted no occasion.

Nor do I claim to comprehend
What Nature has in view
In giving us the very friend
To trust we oughtn't to.
But so it is: The trusty gun
Disastrously exploded
Is always sure to be the one
We didn't think was loaded.

Our moaning is another's mirth,
And what is worse by half,
We say the funniest thing on earth
And never raise a laugh:
Mid friends that love us overwell,
And sparkling jests and liquor,
Our hearts somehow are liable
To melt in tears the quicker.

We reach the wrong when most we seek
The right; in like effect,
We stay the strong and not the weak
Do most when we neglect.
Neglected genius, truth be said
As wild and quick as tinder,
The more we seek to help ahead
The more we seem to hinder.

I've known the least the greatest, too
And, on the selfsame plan,
The biggest fool I ever knew
Was quite a little man:
We find we ought, and then we won't
We prove a thing, then doubt it,
Know everything but when we don't
Know anything about it.


A SCRAWL
I want to sing something but this is all
I try and I try, but the rhymes are dull
As though they were damp, and the echoes fall
Limp and unlovable.

Words will not say what I yearn to say
They will not walk as I want them to,
But they stumble and fall in the path of the way
Of my telling my love for you.

Simply take what the scrawl is worth
Knowing I love you as sun the sod
On the ripening side of the great round earth
That swings in the smile of God.


WRITIN' BACK TO THE HOME-FOLKS
My dear old friends, It jes beats all,
The way you write a letter
So's ever' last line beats the first,

And ever' next-un's better!
W'y, ever' fool-thing you putt down
You make so interestin',
A feller, readin' of 'em all,
Can't tell which is the best-un.

It's all so comfortin' and good,
'Pears-like I almost hear ye
And git more sociabler, you know,
And hitch my cheer up near ye
And jes smile on ye like the sun
Acrosst the whole per-rairies
In Aprile when the thaw's begun
And country couples marries.

It's all so good-old-fashioned like
To talk jes like we're thinkin',
Without no hidin' back o' fans
And giggle-un and winkin',
Ner sizin' how each-other's dressed
Like some is allus doin',
"Is Marthy Ellen's basque ben turned
Er shore-enough a new-un!"

Er "ef Steve's city-friend haint jes
'A leetle kindo'-sorto'"
Er "wears them-air blame eye-glasses
Jes 'cause he hadn't ort to?"
And so straight on, dad-libitum,
Tel all of us feels, someway,
Jes like our "comp'ny" wuz the best
When we git up to come 'way!

That's why I like old friends like you,
Jes 'cause you're so abidin'.
Ef I was built to live "fer keeps,"
My principul residin'
Would be amongst the folks 'at kep'
Me allus thinkin' of 'em,
And sorto' eechin' all the time
To tell 'em how I love 'em.

Sich folks, you know, I jes love so
I wouldn't live without 'em,
Er couldn't even drap asleep
But what I dreamp' about 'em,
And ef we minded God, I guess
We'd all love one-another
Jes like one fam'bly, me and Pap
And Madaline and Mother.

### LAUGHTER HOLDING BOTH HIS SIDES

Ay, thou varlet! Laugh away!
All the world's a holiday!
Laugh away, and roar and shout
Till thy hoarse tongue lolleth out!
Bloat thy cheeks, and bulge thine eyes
Unto bursting; pelt thy thighs
With thy swollen palms, and roar
As thou never hast before!
Lustier! wilt thou! peal on peal!
Stiflest? Squat and grind thy heel
Wrestle with thy loins, and then
Wheeze thee whiles, and whoop again!


### THE SONG OF YESTERDAY

I

But yesterday
I looked away
O'er happy lands, where sunshine lay
In golden blots
Inlaid with spots
Of shade and wild forget-me-nots.

My head was fair
With flaxen hair,
And fragrant breezes, faint and rare,
And warm with drouth
From out the south,
Blew all my curls across my mouth.

And, cool and sweet,
My naked feet
Found dewy pathways through the wheat;
And out again
Where, down the lane,
The dust was dimpled with the rain.

II

But yesterday:
Adream, astray,
From morning's red to evening's gray,
O'er dales and hills
Of daffodils
And lorn sweet-fluting whippoorwills.

I knew nor cares
Nor tears nor prayers

A mortal god, crowned unawares
With sunset and
A scepter-wand
Of apple-blossoms in my hand!

The dewy blue
Of twilight grew
To purple, with a star or two
Whose lisping rays
Failed in the blaze
Of sudden fireflies through the haze.

III

But yesterday
I heard the lay
Of summer birds, when I, as they
With breast and wing,
All quivering
With life and love, could only sing.

My head was lent
Where, with it, blent
A maiden's o'er her instrument;
While all the night,
From vale to height,
Was filled with echoes of delight.

And all our dreams
Were lit with gleams
Of that lost land of reedy streams.
Along whose brim
Forever swim
Pan's lilies, laughing up at him.


IV

But yesterday!...
O blooms of May,
And summer roses where-away?
O stars above;
And lips of love,
And all the honeyed sweets thereof!

O lad and lass,
And orchard pass,
And briered lane, and daisied grass!
O gleam and gloom,
And woodland bloom,
And breezy breaths of all perfume!

No more for me

Or mine shall be
Thy raptures, save in memory,
No more, no more
Till through the Door
Of Glory gleam the days of yore.


SONG OF PARTING

Say farewell, and let me go;
Shatter every vow!
All the future can bestow
Will be welcome now!
And if this fair hand I touch
I have worshipped overmuch,
It was my mistake and so,
Say farewell, and let me go.

Say farewell, and let me go:
Murmur no regret,
Stay your tear-drops ere they flow
Do not waste them yet!
They might pour as pours the rain,
And not wash away the pain:
I have tried them and I know.
Say farewell, and let me go.

Say farewell, and let me go:
Think me not untrue
True as truth is, even so
I am true to you!
If the ghost of love may stay
Where my fond heart dies to-day,
I am with you alway so,
Say farewell, and let me go.


OUR KIND OF A MAN
I
The kind of a man for you and me!
He faces the world unflinchingly,
And smites, as long as the wrong resists,
With a knuckled faith and force like fists:
He lives the life he is preaching of,
And loves where most is the need of love;
His voice is clear to the deaf man's ears,
And his face sublime through the blind man's tears;
The light shines out where the clouds were dim,
And the widow's prayer goes up for him;
The latch is clicked at the hovel door

And the sick man sees the sun once more,
And out o'er the barren fields he sees
Springing blossoms and waving trees,
Feeling as only the dying may,
That God's own servant has come that way,
Smoothing the path as it still winds on
Through the Golden Gate where his loved have gone.

II
The kind of a man for me and you!
However little of worth we do
He credits full, and abides in trust
That time will teach us how more is just.
He walks abroad, and he meets all kinds
Of querulous and uneasy minds,
And, sympathizing, he shares the pain
Of the doubts that rack us, heart and brain;
And, knowing this, as we grasp his hand,
We are surely coming to understand!
He looks on sin with pitying eyes
E'en as the Lord, since Paradise,
Else, should we read, "Though our sins should glow
As scarlet, they shall be white as snow"?
And, feeling still, with a grief half glad,
That the bad are as good as the good are bad,
He strikes straight out for the Right and he
Is the kind of a man for you and me!


"HOW DID YOU REST, LAST NIGHT?"
"How did you rest, last night?"
I've heard my gran'pap say
Them words a thousand times, that's right
Jes them words thataway!
As punctchul-like as morning dast
To ever heave in sight
Gran'pap 'ud allus haf to ast
"How did you rest, last night?"

Us young-uns used to grin,
At breakfast, on the sly,
And mock the wobble of his chin
And eyebrows belt so high
And kind: "How did you rest, last night?"
We'd mumble and let on
Our voices trimbled, and our sight
Was dim, and hearin' gone.

Bad as I used to be,
All I'm a-wantin' is

As puore and ca'm a sleep fer me
And sweet a sleep as his!
And so I pray, on Jedgment Day
To wake, and with its light
See his face dawn, and hear him say
"How did you rest, last night?"


OUT OF THE HITHERWHERE
Out of the hitherwhere into the Yon
The land that the Lord's love rests upon;
Where one may rely on the friends he meets,
And the smiles that greet him along the streets:
Where the mother that left you years ago
Will lift the hands that were folded so,
And put them about you, with all the love
And tenderness you are dreaming of.

Out of the hitherwhere into the Yon
Where all of the friends of your youth have gone,
Where the old schoolmate that laughed with you,
Will laugh again as he used to do,
Running to meet you, with such a face
As lights like a moon the wondrous place
Where God is living, and glad to live,
Since He is the Master and may forgive.

Out of the hitherwhere into the Yon!
Stay the hopes we are leaning on
You, Divine, with Your merciful eyes
Looking down from the far-away skies,
Smile upon us, and reach and take
Our worn souls Home for the old home's sake.
And so Amen, for our all seems gone
Out of the hitherwhere into the Yon.


JACK-IN-THE-BOX
(Grandfather, musing.)

In childish days! O memory,
You bring such curious things to me!
Laughs to the lip, tears to the eye,
In looking on the gifts that lie
Like broken playthings scattered o'er
Imagination's nursery floor!
Did these old hands once click the key
That let "Jack's" box-lid upward fly,
And that blear-eyed, fur-whiskered elf

Leap, as though frightened at himself,
And quiveringly lean and stare
At me, his jailer, laughing there?

A child then! Now, I only know
They call me very old; and so
They will not let me have my way,
But uselessly I sit all day
Here by the chimney-jamb, and poke
The lazy fire, and smoke and smoke,
And watch the wreaths swoop up the flue,
And chuckle ay, I often do
Seeing again, all vividly,
Jack-in-the-box leap, as in glee
To see how much he looks like me!

... They talk. I can't hear what they say
But I am glad, clean through and through
Sometimes, in fancying that they
Are saying, "Sweet, that fancy strays
In age back to our childish days!"


## THE BOYS

Where are they? the friends of my childhood enchanted
The clear, laughing eyes looking back in my own,
And the warm, chubby fingers my palms have so wanted,
As when we raced over
Pink pastures of clover,
And mocked the quail's whir and the bumblebee's drone?

Have the breezes of time blown their blossomy faces
Forever adrift down the years that are flown?
Am I never to see them romp back to their places,
Where over the meadow,
In sunshine and shadow,
The meadow-larks trill, and the bumblebees drone?

Where are they? Ah! dim in the dust lies the clover;
The whippoorwill's call has a sorrowful tone,
And the dove's I have wept at it over and over;
I want the glad luster
Of youth, and the cluster
Of faces asleep where the bumblebees drone!


## IT'S GOT TO BE

"When it's got to be," like! always say,
As I notice the years whiz past,

And know each day is a yesterday,
When we size it up, at last,
Same as I said when my boyhood went
And I knowed we had to quit,
"It's got to be, and it's goin' to be!"
So I said "Good-by" to it.

It's got to be, and it's goin' to be!
So at least I always try
To kind o' say in a hearty way,
"Well, it's got to be. Good-by!"

The time jes melts like a late, last snow,
When it's got to be, it melts!
But I aim to keep a cheerful mind,
Ef I can't keep nothin' else!
I knowed, when I come to twenty-one,
That I'd soon be twenty-two,
So I waved one hand at the soft young man,
And I said, "Good-by to you!"

It's got to be, and it's goin' to be!
So at least I always try
To kind o' say, in a cheerful way,
"Well, it's got to be. Good-by!"

They kep' a-goin', the years and years,
Yet still I smiled and smiled,
For I'd said "Good-by" to my single life,
And I now had a wife and child:
Mother and son and the father one,
Till, last, on her bed of pain,
She jes' smiled up, like she always done,
And I said "Good-by" again.

It's got to be, and it's goin' to be!
So at least I always try
To kind o' say, in a humble way,
"Well, it's got to be. Good-by!"

And then my boy as he growed to be
Almost a man in size,
Was more than a pride and joy to me,
With his mother's smilin' eyes.
He gimme the slip, when the War broke out,
And followed me. And I
Never knowed till the first right's end ...
I found him, and then, ... "Good-by."

It's got to be, and it's goin' to be!
So at least I always try

To kind o' say, in a patient way,
"Well, it's got to be. Good-by!"

I have said, "Good-by! Good-by! Good-by!"
With my very best good will,
All through life from the first, and I
Am a cheerful old man still:

But it's got to end, and it's goin' to end!
And this is the thing I'll do,
With my last breath I will laugh, O Death,
And say "Good-by" to you!...

It's got to be! And again I say,
When his old scythe circles high,
I'll laugh of course, in the kindest way,
As I say "Good-by! Good-by!"


"OUT OF REACH?"
You think them "out of reach," your dead?
Nay, by my own dead, I deny
Your "out of reach." Be comforted:
'Tis not so far to die.

O by their dear remembered smiles
And outheld hands and welcoming speech,
They wait for us, thousands of miles
This side of "out-of-reach."


"A BRAVE REFRAIN"
When snow is here, and the trees look weird,
And the knuckled twigs are gloved with frost;
When the breath congeals in the drover's beard,
And the old pathway to the barn is lost;
When the rooster's crow is sad to hear,
And the stamp of the stabled horse is vain,
And the tone of the cow-bell grieves the ear
O then is the time for a brave refrain!

When the gears hang stiff on the harness-peg,
And the tallow gleams in frozen streaks;
And the old hen stands on a lonesome leg,
And the pump sounds hoarse and the handle squeaks;
When the woodpile lies in a shrouded heap,
And the frost is scratched from the window-pane
And anxious eyes from the inside peep
O then is the time for a brave refrain!

When the ax-helve warms at the chimney-jamb,
And hob-nailed shoes on the hearth below,
And the house-cat curls in a slumber calm,
And the eight-day clock ticks loud and slow;
When the harsh broom-handle jabs the ceil
'Neath the kitchen-loft, and the drowsy brain
Sniffs the breath of the morning meal
O then is the time for a brave refrain!

ENVOI
When the skillet seethes, and a blubbering hot
Tilts the lid of the coffee-pot,
And the scent of the buckwheat cake grows plain
O then is the time for a brave refrain!


IN THE EVENING
I

In the evening of our days,
When the first far stars above
Glimmer dimmer, through the haze,
Than the dewy eyes of love,
Shall we mournfully revert
To the vanished morns and Mays
Of our youth, with hearts that hurt,
In the evening of our days?

II
Shall the hand that holds your own
Till the twain are thrilled as now,
Be withheld, or colder grown?
Shall my kiss upon your brow
Falter from its high estate?
And, in all forgetful ways,
Shall we sit apart and wait
In the evening of our days?

III
Nay, my wife, my life! the gloom
Shall enfold us velvetwise,
And my smile shall be the groom
Of the gladness of your eyes:
Gently, gently as the dew
Mingles with the darkening maze,
I shall fall asleep with you
In the evening of our days.

JIM

He was jes a plain, ever'-day, all-round kind of a jour.,
Consumpted-lookin' but la!
The jokiest, wittiest, story-tellin', song-singin', laughin'est, jolliest
Feller you ever saw!
Worked at jes coarse work, but you kin bet he was fine enough in his talk,
And his feelin's, too!
Lordy! ef he was on'y back on his bench ag'in to-day, a-carryin' on
Like he ust to do!

Any shop-mate'll tell you there never was, on top o' dirt,
A better feller'n Jim!
You want a favor, and couldn't git it anywheres else
You could git it o' him!
Most free-heartedest man thataway in the world, I guess!
Give up ever' nickel he's worth
And, ef you'd-a-wanted it, and named it to him, and it was his,
He'd a-give you the earth!

Allus a-reachin' out, Jim was, and a-he'ppin' some
Pore feller onto his feet
He'd a-never a-keered how hungry he was hisse'f,
So's the feller got somepin' to eat!
Didn't make no differ'nee at all to him how he was dressed,
He ust to say to me,
"You togg out a tramp purty comfortable in winter-time, a-huntin' a job,
And he'll git along!" says he.

Jim didn't have, ner never could git ahead, so overly much
O' this world's goods at a time.
'Fore now I've saw him, more'n one't, lend a dollar, and haf to, more'n like,
Turn round and borry a dime!
Mebby laugh and joke about it hisse'f fer a while, then jerk his coat.
And kindo' square his chin,
Tie on his apern, and squat hisse'f on his old shoe-bench,
And go to peggin' ag'in!

Patientest feller, too, I reckon, 'at ever jes natchurly
Coughed hisse'f to death!
Long enough after his voice was lost he'd laugh in a whisper and say
He could git ever'thing but his breath
"You fellers," he'd sorto' twinkle his eyes and say,
"Is a-pilin' onto me
A mighty big debt fer that-air little weak-chested ghost o' mine to pack
Through all Eternity!"

Now there was a man 'at jes 'peared-like, to me,
'At ortn't a-never a-died!
"But death hain't a-showin' no favors," the old boss said
"On'y to Jim!" and cried:
And Wigger, who puts up the best sewed-work in the shop

Er the whole blame neighborhood,
He says, "When God made Jim, I bet you He didn't do anything else that day
But jes set around and feel good!"


## THE BEST IS GOOD ENOUGH
I quarrel not with Destiny,
But make the best of everything
The best is good enough for me.

Leave Discontent alone, and she
Will shut her month and let you sing.
I quarrel not with Destiny.

I take some things, or let 'em be
Good gold has always got the ring;
The best is good enough for me.

Since Fate insists on secrecy,
I have no arguments to bring
quarrel not with Destiny.

The fellow that goes "haw" for "gee"
Will find he hasn't got full swing.
The best is good enough for me.

One only knows our needs, and He
Does all of the distributing.
I quarrel not with Destiny;
The best is good enough for me.


## HONEY DRIPPING FROM THE COMB
How slight a thing may set one's fancy drifting
Upon the dead sea of the Past! A view
Sometimes an odor or a rooster lifting
A far-off "Ooh! ooh-ooh!"

And suddenly we find ourselves astray
In some wood's-pasture of the Long Ago
Or idly dream again upon a day
Of rest we used to know.

I bit an apple but a moment since
A wilted apple that the worm had spurned.
Yet hidden in the taste were happy hints
Of good old days returned.

And so my heart, like some enraptured lute,

Tinkles a tune so tender and complete,
God's blessing must be resting on the fruit
So bitter, yet so sweet!


AS MY UNCLE USED TO SAY
I've thought a power on men and things,
As my uncle ust to say,
And ef folks don't work as they pray, i jings!
W'y, they ain't no use to pray!
Ef you want somepin', and jes dead-set
A-pleadin' fer it with both eyes wet,
And tears won't bring it, w'y, you try sweat,
As my uncle ust to say.

They's some don't know their A, B, C's,
As my uncle ust to say,
And yit don't waste no candle-grease,
Ner whistle their lives away!
But ef they can't write no book, ner rhyme
No singin' song fer to last all time,
They can blaze the way fer the march sublime,
As my uncle ust to say.

Whoever's Foreman of all things here,
As my uncle ust to say,
He knows each job 'at we're best fit fer,
And our round-up, night and day:
And a-sizin' His work, east and west,
And north and south, and worst and best.
I ain't got nothin' to suggest,
As my uncle ust to say.


WE MUST BELIEVE
"Lord, I believe: help Thou mine unbelief."

We must believe
Being from birth endowed with love and trust
Born unto loving; and how simply just
That love, that faith! even in the blossom-face
The babe drops dreamward in its resting-place,
Intuitively conscious of the sure
Awakening to rapture ever pure
And sweet and saintly as the mother's own,
Or the awed father's, as his arms are thrown
O'er wife and child, to round about them weave
And wind and bind them as one harvest-sheaf
Of love, to cleave to, and forever cleave....

Lord, I believe:
Help Thou mine unbelief.

We must believe
Impelled since infancy to seek some clear
Fulfillment, still withheld all seekers here;
For never have we seen perfection nor
The glory we are ever seeking for:
But we have seen, all mortal souls as one
Have seen its promise, in the morning sun
Its blest assurance, in the stars of night;
The ever-dawning of the dark to light;
The tears down-falling from all eyes that grieve
The eyes uplifting from all deeps of grief,
Yearning for what at last we shall receive....
Lord, I believe:
Help Thou mine unbelief.

We must believe
For still all unappeased our hunger goes,
From life's first waking, to its last repose:
The briefest life of any babe, or man
Outwearing even the allotted span,
Is each a life unfinished, incomplete:
For these, then, of th' outworn, or unworn feet
Denied one toddling step, O there must be
Some fair, green, flowery pathway endlessly
Winding through lands Elysian! Lord, receive
And lead each as Thine Own Child, even the Chief
Of us who didst Immortal life achieve....
Lord, I believe:
Help Thou mine unbelief.


A GOOD MAN

I

A good man never dies
In worthy deed and prayer
And helpful hands, and honest eyes,
If smiles or tears be there:
Who lives for you and me
Lives for the world he tries
To help, he lives eternally.
A good man never dies.

II

Who lives to bravely take
His share of toil and stress,
And, for his weaker fellows' sake,
Makes every burden less,

He may, at last, seem worn
Lie fallen, hands and eyes
Folded, yet, though we mourn and mourn,
A good man never dies.


THE OLD DAYS
The old days, the far days
The overdear and fair!
The old days, the lost days
How lovely they were!
The old days of Morning,
With the dew-drench on the flowers
And apple-buds and blossoms
Of those old days of ours.

Then was the real gold
Spendthrift Summer flung;
Then was the real song
Bird or Poet sung!
There was never censure then,
Only honest praise
And all things were worthy of it
In the old days.

There bide the true friends
The first and the best;
There clings the green grass
Close where they rest:
Would they were here? No;
Would we were there!...
The old days, the lost days
How lovely they were!


A SPRING SONG AND A LATER
She sang a song of May for me,
Wherein once more I heard
The mirth of my glad infancy
The orchard's earliest bird
The joyous breeze among the trees
New-clad in leaf and bloom,
And there the happy honey-bees
In dewy gleam and gloom.

So purely, sweetly on the sense
Of heart and spirit fell
Her song of Spring, its influence
Still irresistible,

Commands me here, with eyes ablur
To mate her bright refrain.
Though I but shed a rhyme for her
As dim as Autumn rain.


### KNEELING WITH HERRICK

Dear Lord, to Thee my knee is bent
Give me content
Full-pleasured with what comes to me,
Whate'er it be:
An humble roof, a frugal board,
And simple hoard;
The wintry fagot piled beside
The chimney wide,
While the enwreathing flames up-sprout
And twine about
The brazen dogs that guard my hearth
And household worth:
Tinge with the ember's ruddy glow
The rafters low;
And let the sparks snap with delight,
As fingers might
That mark deft measures of some tune
The children croon:
Then, with good friends, the rarest few
Thou boldest true,
Ranged round about the blaze, to share
My comfort there,
Give me to claim the service meet
That makes each seat
A place of honor, and each guest
Loved as the rest.


### THE RAINY MORNING

The dawn of the day was dreary,
And the lowering clouds o'erhead
Wept in a silent sorrow
Where the sweet sunshine lay dead;
And a wind came out of the eastward
Like an endless sigh of pain,
And the leaves fell down in the pathway
And writhed in the falling rain.

I had tried in a brave endeavor
To chord my harp with the sun,
But the strings would slacken ever,
And the task was a weary one:

And so, like a child impatient
And sick of a discontent,
I bowed in a shower of teardrops
And mourned with the instrument.

And lo! as I bowed, the splendor
Of the sun bent over me,
With a touch as warm and tender
As a father's hand might be:
And even as I felt its presence,
My clouded soul grew bright,
And the tears, like the rain of morning,
Melted in mists of light.


## REACH YOUR HAND TO ME

Reach your hand to me, my friend,
With its heartiest caress
Sometime there will come an end
To its present faithfulness
Sometime I may ask in vain
For the touch of it again,
When between us land or sea
Holds it ever back from me.

Sometime I may need it so,
Groping somewhere in the night,
It will seem to me as though
Just a touch, however light,
Would make all the darkness day,
And along some sunny way
Lead me through an April-shower
Of my tears to this fair hour.

O the present is too sweet
To go on forever thus!
Round the corner of the street
Who can say what waits for us?
Meeting, greeting, night and day,
Faring each the selfsame way
Still somewhere the path must end.
Reach your hand to me, my friend!


## TO MY OLD FRIEND, WILLIAM LEACHMAN

Fer forty year and better you have been a friend to me,
Through days of sore afflictions and dire adversity,
You allus had a kind word of counsul to impart,
Which was like a healin' 'intment to the sorrow of my hart.

When I burried my first womern, William Leachman, it was you
Had the only consolation that I could listen to
Fer I knowed you had gone through it and had rallied from the blow,
And when you said I'd do the same, I knowed you'd ort to know.

But that time I'll long remember; how I wundered here and thare
Through the settin'-room and kitchen, and out in the open air
And the snowflakes whirlin', whirlin', and the fields a frozen glare,
And the neghbors' sleds and wagons congergatin' ev'rywhare.

I turned my eyes to'rds heaven, but the sun was hid away;
I turned my eyes to'rds earth again, but all was cold and gray;
And the clock, like ice a-crackin', clickt the icy hours in two
And my eyes'd never thawed out ef it hadn't been fer you!

We set thare by the smoke-house, me and you out thare alone
Me a-thinkin', you a-talkin' in a soothin' undertone
You a-talkin', me a-thinkin' of the summers long ago,
And a-writin' "Marthy, Marthy" with my finger in the snow!

William Leachman, I can see you jest as plane as I could then;
And your hand is on my shoulder, and you rouse me up again,
And I see the tears a-drippin' from your own eyes, as you say:
"Be rickonciled and bear it, we but linger fer a day!"

At the last Old Settlers' Meetin' we went j'intly, you and me
Your hosses and my wagon, as you wanted it to be;
And sence I can remember, from the time we've neghbored here,
In all sich friendly actions you have double-done your sheer.

It was better than the meetin', too, that nine-mile talk we had
Of the times when we first settled here and travel was so bad;
When we had to go on hoss-back, and sometimes on "Shanks's mare,"
And "blaze" a road fer them behind that had to travel thare.

And now we was a-trottin' 'long a level gravel pike,
In a big two-hoss road-wagon, jest as easy as you like
Two of us on the front seat, and our wimmern-folks behind,
A-settin' in theyr Winsor-cheers in perfect peace of mind!

And we pinted out old landmarks, nearly faded out of sight:
Thare they ust to rob the stage-coach; thare Gash Morgan had the fight
With the old stag-deer that pronged him, how he battled fer his life,
And lived to prove the story by the handle of his knife.

Thare the first griss-mill was put up in the Settlement, and we
Had tuck our grindin' to it in the Fall of Forty-three
When we tuck our rifles with us, techin' elbows all the way,
And a-stickin' right together ev'ry minute, night and day.

Thare ust to stand the tavern that they called the "Travelers' Rest,"
And thare, beyent the covered bridge, "The Counter-fitters' Nest"
Whare they claimed the house was ha'nted, that a man was murdered thare,
And burried underneath the floor, er 'round the place somewhare.

And the old Plank-road they laid along in Fifty-one er two
You know we talked about the times when that old road was new:
How "Uncle Sam" put down that road and never taxed the State
Was a problem, don't you rickollect, we couldn't dim-onstrate?

Ways was devius, William Leachman, that me and you has past;
But as I found you true at first, I find you true at last;
And, now the time's a-comin' mighty nigh our jurney's end,
I want to throw wide open all my soul to you, my friend.

With the stren'th of all my bein', and the heat of hart and brane,
And ev'ry livin' drop of blood in artery and vane,
I love you and respect you, and I venerate your name,
Fer the name of William Leachman and True Manhood's jest the same!


## A BACKWARD LOOK

As I sat smoking, alone, yesterday,
And lazily leaning back in my chair,
Enjoying myself in a general way
Allowing my thoughts a holiday
From weariness, toil and care,
My fancies, doubtless, for ventilation
Left ajar the gates of my mind,
And Memory, seeing the situation,
Slipped out in street of "Auld Lang Syne."

Wandering ever with tireless feet
Through scenes of silence, and jubilee
Of long-hushed voices; and faces sweet
Were thronging the shadowy side of the street
As far as the eye could see;
Dreaming again, in anticipation,
The same old dreams of our boyhood's days
That never come true, from the vague sensation
Of walking asleep in the world's strange ways.

Away to the house where I was born!
And there was the selfsame clock that ticked
From the close of dusk to the burst of morn,
When life-warm hands plucked the golden corn
And helped when the apples were picked.
And the "chany-dog" on the mantel-shelf,
With the gilded collar and yellow eyes,
Looked just as at first, when I hugged myself

Sound asleep with the dear surprise.

And down to the swing in the locust tree,
Where the grass was worn from the trampled ground
And where "Eck" Skinner, "Old" Carr, and three
Or four such other boys used to be
Doin' "sky-scrapers," or "whirlin' round:"
And again Bob climbed for the bluebird's nest,
And again "had shows" in the buggy-shed
Of Guymon's barn, where still, unguessed,
The old ghosts romp through the best days dead!

And again I gazed from the old school-room
With a wistful look of a long June day,
When on my cheek was the hectic bloom
Caught of Mischief, as I presume
He had such a "partial" way,
It seemed, toward me. And again I thought
Of a probable likelihood to be
Kept in after school for a girl was caught
Catching a note from me.

And down through the woods to the swimming-hole
Where the big, white, hollow, old sycamore grows,
And we never cared when the water was cold.
And always "clucked" the boy that told
On the fellow that tied the clothes.
When life went so like a dreamy rhyme
That it seems to me now that then
The world was having a jollier time
Than it ever will have again.


### AT SEA

O we go down to sea in ships
But Hope remains behind,
And Love, with laughter on his lips,
And Peace, of passive mind;
While out across the deeps of night,
With lifted sails of prayer,
We voyage off in quest of light,
Nor find it anywhere.

O Thou who wroughtest earth and sea,
Yet keepest from our eyes
The shores of an eternity
In calms of Paradise,
Blow back upon our foolish quest
With all the driving rain
Of blinding tears and wild unrest,

And waft us home again.


## THE OLD GUITAR
Neglected now is the old guitar
And moldering into decay;
Fretted with many a rift and scar
That the dull dust hides away,
While the spider spins a silver star
In its silent lips to-day.

The keys hold only nerveless strings
The sinews of brave old airs
Are pulseless now; and the scarf that clings
So closely here declares
A sad regret in its ravelings
And the faded hue it wears.

But the old guitar, with a lenient grace,
Has cherished a smile for me;
And its features hint of a fairer face
That comes with a memory
Of a flower-and-perfume-haunted place
And a moonlit balcony.

Music sweeter than words confess
Or the minstrel's powers invent,
Thrilled here once at the light caress
Of the fairy hands that lent
This excuse for the kiss I press
On the dear old instrument.

The rose of pearl with the jeweled stem
Still blooms; and the tiny sets
In the circle all are here; the gem
In the keys, and the silver frets;
But the dainty fingers that danced o'er them
Alas for the heart's regrets!

Alas for the loosened strings to-day,
And the wounds of rift and scar
On a worn old heart, with its roundelay
Enthralled with a stronger bar
That Fate weaves on, through a dull decay
Like that of the old guitar!


## JOHN McKEEN
John McKeen, in his rusty dress,

His loosened collar, and swarthy throat;
His face unshaven, and none the less,
His hearty laugh and his wholesomeness,
And the wealth of a workman's vote!

Bring him, O Memory, here once more,
And tilt him back in his Windsor chair
By the kitchen-stove, when the day is o'er
And the light of the hearth is across the floor,
And the crickets everywhere!

And let their voices be gladly blent
With a watery jingle of pans and spoons,
And a motherly chirrup of sweet content,
And neighborly gossip and merriment,
And old-time fiddle-tunes!

Tick the clock with a wooden sound,
And fill the hearing with childish glee
Of rhyming riddle, or story found
In the Robinson Crusoe, leather-bound
Old book of the Used-to-be!

John McKeen of the Past! Ah, John,
To have grown ambitious in worldly ways!
To have rolled your shirt-sleeves down, to don
A broadcloth suit, and, forgetful, gone
Out on election days!

John, ah, John! did it prove your worth
To yield you the office you still maintain?
To fill your pockets, but leave the dearth
Of all the happier things on earth
To the hunger of heart and brain?

Under the dusk of your villa trees,
Edging the drives where your blooded span
Paw the pebbles and wait your ease,
Where are the children about your knees,
And the mirth, and the happy man?

The blinds of your mansion are battened to;
Your faded wife is a close recluse;
And your "finished" daughters will doubtless do
Dutifully all that is willed of you,
And marry as you shall choose!

But O for the old-home voices, blent
With the watery jingle of pans and spoons,
And the motherly chirrup of glad content,
And neighborly gossip and merriment,

And the old-time fiddle-tunes!


THROUGH SLEEPY-LAND
Where do you go when you go to sleep,
Little Boy! Little Boy! where?
'Way 'way in where's Little Bo-Peep,
And Little Boy Blue, and the Cows and Sheep
A-wandering 'way in there; in there
A-wandering 'way in there!

And what do you see when lost in dreams,
Little Boy, 'way in there?
Firefly-glimmers and glowworm-gleams,
And silvery, low, slow-sliding streams,
And mermaids, smiling out, 'way in where
They're a-hiding, 'way in there!

Where do you go when the Fairies call,
Little Boy! Little Boy! where?
Wade through the clews of the grasses tall,
Hearing the weir and the waterfall
And the Wee Folk, 'way in there, in there
And the Kelpies, 'way in there!

And what do you do when you wake at dawn,
Little Boy! Little Boy! what?
Hug my Mommy and kiss her on
Her smiling eyelids, sweet and wan,
And tell her everything I've forgot
About, a-wandering 'way in there
Through the blind-world 'way in there!


"THEM OLD CHEERY WORDS"
Pap he allus ust to say,
"Chris'mus comes but onc't a year!"
Liked to hear him that-a-way,
In his old split-bottomed cheer
By the fireplace here at night
Wood all in, and room all bright,
Warm and snug, and folks all here:
"Chris'mus comes but onc't a year!"

Me and 'Lize, and Warr'n and Jess
And Eldory home fer two
Weeks' vacation; and, I guess,
Old folks tickled through and through,
Same as we was, "Home onc't more

Fer another Chris'mus shore!"
Pap 'u'd say, and tilt his cheer,
"Chris'mus comes but onc't a year!"

Mostly Pap was ap' to be
Ser'ous in his "daily walk,"
As he called it; giner'ly
Was no hand to joke er talk.
Fac's is, Pap had never be'n
Rugged-like at all and then
Three years in the army had
Hepped to break him purty bad.

Never flinched! but frost and snow
Hurt his wownd in winter. But
You bet Mother knowed it, though!
Watched his feet, and made him putt
On his flannen; and his knee,
Where it never healed up, he
Claimed was "well now mighty near
Chris'mus comes but onc't a year!"

"Chris'mus comes but onc't a year!"
Pap 'u'd say, and snap his eyes ...
Row o' apples sputter'n' here
Round the hearth, and me and 'Lize
Crackin' hicker'-nuts; and Warr'n
And Eldory parchin' corn;
And whole raft o' young folks here.
"Chris'mus comes but onc't a year!"

Mother tuk most comfort in
Jest a-heppin' Pap: She'd fill
His pipe fer him, er his tin
O' hard cider; er set still
And read fer him out the pile
O' newspapers putt on file
Whilse he was with Sherman (She
Knowed the whole war-history!)

Sometimes he'd git het up some.
"Boys," he'd say, "and you girls, too,
Chris'mus is about to come;
So, as you've a right to do,
Celebrate it! Lots has died,
Same as Him they crucified,
That you might be happy here.
Chris'mus comes but onc't a year!"

Missed his voice last Chris'mus missed
Them old cheery words, you know.

Mother belt up tel she kissed
All of us then had to go
And break down! And I laughs: "Here!
'Chris'mus comes but onc't a year!"
"Them's his very words," sobbed she,
"When he asked to marry me."

"Chris'mus comes but onc't a year!"
"Chris'mus comes but onc't a year!"
Over, over, still I hear,
"Chris'mus comes but onc't a year!"
Yit, like him, I'm goin' to smile
And keep cheerful all the while:
Allus Chris'mus There And here
"Chris'mus comes but onc't a year!"


TO THE JUDGE
A Voice From the Interior of Old Hoop-Pole Township

Friend of my earliest youth,
Can't you arrange to come down
And visit a fellow out here in the woods
Out of the dust of the town?
Can't you forget you're a Judge
And put by your dolorous frown
And tan your wan face in the smile of a friend
Can't you arrange to come down?

Can't you forget for a while
The arguments prosy and drear,
To lean at full-length in indefinite rest
In the lap of the greenery here?
Can't you kick over "the Bench,"
And "husk" yourself out of your gown
To dangle your legs where the fishing is good
Can't you arrange to come down?

Bah! for your office of State!
And bah! for its technical lore!
What does our President, high in his chair,
But wish himself low as before!
Pick between peasant and king,
Poke your bald head through a crown
Or shadow it here with the laurels of Spring!
Can't you arrange to come down?

"Judge it" out here, if you will,
The birds are in session by dawn;
You can draw, not complaints, but a sketch of the hill

And a breath that your betters have drawn;
You can open your heart, like a case,
To a jury of kine, white and brown,
And their verdict of "Moo" will just satisfy you!
Can't you arrange to come down?

Can't you arrange it, old Pard?
Pigeonhole Blackstone and Kent!
Here we have "Breitmann," and Ward,
Twain, Burdette, Nye, and content!
Can't you forget you're a Judge
And put by your dolorous frown
And tan your wan face in the smile of a friend
Can't you arrange to come down?


## OUR BOYHOOD HAUNTS

Ho! I'm going back to where
We were youngsters. Meet me there,
Dear old barefoot chum, and we
Will be as we used to be,
Lawless rangers up and down
The old creek beyond the town
Little sunburnt gods at play,
Just as in that far-away:
Water nymphs, all unafraid,
Shall smile at us from the brink
Of the old millrace and wade
Tow'rd us as we kneeling drink
At the spring our boyhood knew,
Pure and clear as morning-dew:

And, as we are rising there,
Doubly dow'rd to hear and see,
We shall thus be made aware
Of an eerie piping, heard
High above the happy bird
In the hazel: And then we,
Just across the creek, shall see
(Hah! the goaty rascal!) Pan
Hoof it o'er the sloping green,
Mad with his own melody,
Aye, and (bless the beasty man!)
Stamping from the grassy soil
Bruiséd scents of fleur-de-lis,
Boneset, mint and pennyroyal.


## MY DANCIN'-DAYS IS OVER

What is it in old fiddle-chunes 'at makes me ketch my breath
And ripples up my backbone tel I'm tickled most to death?
Kindo' like that sweet-sick feelin', in the long sweep of a swing,
The first you ever swung in, with yer first sweet-heart, i jing!
Yer first picnic, yer first ice-cream, yer first o' ever'thing
'At happened 'fore yer dancin'-days wuz over!

I never understood it, and I s'pose I never can,
But right in town here, yisterd'y, I heerd a pore blindman
A-fiddlin' old "Gray Eagle" And-sir! I jes stopped my load
O' hay and listened at him, yes, and watched the way he "bow'd,"
And back I went, plum forty year', with boys and girls I knowed
And loved, long 'fore my dancin'-days wuz over!

At high noon in yer city, with yer blame Magnetic-Cars
A-hummin' and a-screetchin' past and bands and G.A.R.'s
A-marchin' and fire-ingines. All the noise, the whole street through,
Wuz lost on me! I only heerd a whipperwill er two,
It 'peared-like, kindo' callin' 'crost the darkness and the dew,
Them nights afore my dancin'-days wuz over.

T'uz Chused'y-night at Wetherell's, er We'nsd'y-night at Strawn's,
Er Fourth-o'-July-night at uther Tomps's house er John's!
With old Lew Church from Sugar Crick, with that old fiddle he
Had sawed clean through the Army, from Atlanty to the sea
And yit he'd fetched, her home ag'in, so's he could play fer me
One't more afore my dancin'-days wuz over!

The woods 'at's all ben cut away wuz growin' same as then;
The youngsters all wuz boys ag'in 'at's now all oldish men;
And all the girls 'at then wuz girls, I saw 'em, one and all,
As plain as then, the middle-sized, the short-and-fat, and tall
And, 'peared-like, I danced "Tucker" fer 'em up and down the wall
Jes like afore my dancin' days wuz over!

Yer po-leece they can holler "Say! you, Uncle! drive ahead!
You can't use all the right-o'-way!", fer that wuz what they said!
But, jes the same, in spite of all 'at you call "interprise
And prog-gress of you-folks Today," we're all of fambly-ties
We're all got feelin's fittin' fer the tears 'at's in our eyes
Er the smiles afore our dancin'-days is over.


HER BEAUTIFUL HANDS
O your hands, they are strangely fair!
Fair, for the jewels that sparkle there,
Fair, for the witchery of the spell
That ivory keys alone can tell;
But when their delicate touches rest
Here in my own do I love them best,

As I clasp with eager acquisitive spans
My glorious treasure of beautiful hands!

Marvelous, wonderful, beautiful hands!
They can coax roses to bloom in the strands
Of your brown tresses; and ribbons will twine.
Under mysterious touches of thine,
Into such knots as entangle the soul,
And fetter the heart under such a control
As only the strength of my love understands
My passionate love for your beautiful hands.

As I remember the first fair touch
Of those beautiful hands that I love so much,
I seem to thrill as I then was thrilled,
Kissing the glove that I found unfilled
When I met your gaze, and the queenly bow,
As you said to me, laughingly, "Keep it now!"
And dazed and alone in a dream I stand
Kissing this ghost of your beautiful hand.

When first I loved, in the long ago,
And held your hand as I told you so
Pressed and caressed it and gave it a kiss,
And said "I could die for a hand like this!"
Little I dreamed love's fulness yet
Had to ripen when eyes were wet,
And prayers were vain in their wild demands
For one warm touch of your beautiful hands.

Beautiful Hands! O Beautiful Hands!
Could you reach out of the alien lands
Where you are lingering, and give me, to-night,
Only a touch, were it ever so light
My heart were soothed, and my weary brain
Would lull itself into rest again;
For there is no solace the world commands
Like the caress of your beautiful hands.

### James Whitcomb Riley – A Short Biography

Poet and author James Whitcomb Riley was born on October 7th 1849 in Greenfield, Indiana. Known as the "Hoosier Poet" for his work with regional dialects, and as the "Children's Poet" for his children's poetry and devotion to youth causes, Riley is best remembered as the author of the well-loved verse book, *Rhymes of Childhood*.

Riley grew up in a well-off and influential family. Riley's father, Reuben Andrew Riley, was a lawyer and Democrat member of the Indiana House of Representatives and he named his son for his friend James Whitcomb, then the governor of Indiana.

Riley had a spotty education, learning at home and attending his local school sporadically (he did not graduate Grade 8 until the age of twenty). Nonetheless, his was a childhood full of creativity. He learned about poetry from an uncle who was a poet and enthusiast and was encouraged by his mother to write and produce juvenile theatrical presentations. His father taught him how to play the guitar and Riley went on to perform in a local band.

Life changed when Riley's father went off to fight in the Civil War in 1861. The family (which already included six children) took in an additional orphan child and suffered many hardships. Riley would base his famous poem, *Little Orphant Annie* on this temporary foster sibling (both the child and the poem were named "Allie", but a typesetter made a crucial typo when the poem was finally published).

Riley Senior returned from soldiering a broken man, partially paralyzed and unable to resume his practice. The family was forced to sell their house in town and retreated to the family farm where Riley's mother died in 1870. Riley became estranged from his father at this time and left home. He also started drinking excessively, beginning a life-long habit that would both impact his health and his career.

He embarked on a series of low-paying jobs – house painting, Bible salesman – before starting a sign-painting business in Greenfield. Riley wrote catchy slogans for his signs, in effect, his first published verses. He also started participating in local theatre productions and sending poems to the *Indianapolis Mirror* under the pseudonym "Jay Whit".

When he went to work for the McGrillus Company in Anderson, Indiana shilling tonic medicines in a travelling show that visited small towns around the state, he discovered another calling. Riley both wrote and performed skits promoting the tonics. Eventually, Riley and several friends started a billboard company that became successful enough that he was able to turn to writing in a more committed way, and he returned to Greenfield to do so.

Riley started sending out dozens of poems to newspapers around the country and many of them – the *Danbury News*, the *Indianapolis Journal* and the *Anderson Democrat*, among them – published the verses. At the same time, Riley began to write to prominent American writers, sending poems and requesting their endorsement. He was successful with poet Henry Wadsworth Longfellow who wrote back, "I have read the poems with great pleasure, and I think they show a true poetic faculty and insight." Riley would finally meet Longfellow in person shortly before the latter's death in 1882; he famously wrote about the experience and about Longfellow's profound impact on his work.

The *Anderson Democrat* offered Riley a reporting job in 1877. He took it on while continuing to submit poems at journals and newspapers all over the country. Riley would lose the stability of this reporting job when a prank in which he submitted a poem to a journal claiming it was Edgar Allan Poe's went awry. Spurned by many publishers after this embarrassing incident, Riley joined a travelling lecture circuit and gave poetry readings around the state. A born entertainer, Riley's readings would become hugely popular and remained a primary source of income for most of his life.

Eventually, the Poe debacle faded into the background and the *Indianapolis Journal* relented, hiring Riley as a columnist in 1879; he wrote regularly for them about society affairs while continuing to tour his increasingly theatrical and comedic poetry readings. As his fame increased, Riley dropped his "Jay Whit" pseudonym and wrote under his own name from about 1881.

Around this time Riley began writing what are known as his "Boone County poems". They are almost entirely written in dialect and emphasize rural and agricultural topics, often evoking nostalgia for the simplicity of country life. *The Old Swimmin'-Hole* and *When the Frost Is on the Punkin'* were the most popular, and helped earn the entire series critical acclaim. In 1883, a friend arranged for the private publication of *The Old Swimmin' Hole and 'Leven More Poems'*. The book's popularity dictated a second printing before the end of the year and it continued to sell for years, bolstered by Riley's reading tours.

Riley's prose style lent itself well to public performance. With their emphasis on the natural speech rhythms of mid-western dialects, his most famous poems – *Raggedy Man*, *Little Orphant Annie* – can look slightly ridiculous on the page. But they come alive when read aloud:

*Little Orphant Annie's come to our house to stay,*
*An' wash the cups an' saucers up, an' brush the crumbs away,*
*An' shoo the chickens off the porch, an' dust the hearth, an'sweep,*
*An' make the fire, an' bake the bread, an' earn her board-an'-keep;*
*An' all us other childern, when the supper-things is done,*
*We set around the kitchen fire an' has the mostest fun*
*A-list'nin' to the witch-tales 'at Annie tells about,*
*An' the Gobble-uns 'at gits you*
*Ef you*
*Don't*
*Watch*
*Out!*

This phenomenon is likely the key to Riley's success with children's verse, as well as the reason he was able to build such fame and fortune on the travelling lecture circuit. It helped also that he was a confident and talented performer.

In 1881 Riley was invited to tour with the Redpath Lyceum Circuit, a prominent series that included writers such as Ralph Waldo Emerson on its roster of regular lecturers. After a successful first season reading in Chicago and Indianapolis, Riley signed a ten-year contract with the Circuit and embarked on a tour of the Eastern seaboard starting in Boston. Riley toured with the Circuit until 1885 when he joined forces with humourist Edgar Wilson Nye. In 1888, the pair co-wrote *Nye and Riley's Railway Guide*, a collection of poems and anecdotes. Nye and Riley also teamed up with another famous American humourist Samuel Clemons (Mark Twain) for joint performances in New York City. Despite contract and agent woes that deprived Riley of his full share of the proceeds, he continued touring with Nye through 1890.

Riley published his third compilation of work in 1888. *Old-Fashioned Roses* was written specifically for the British market and consisted mostly of sonnets; Riley intentionally left his country bumpkin dialects out of this collection. The book was a predictable success in the UK and Riley travelled to Scotland (where he made a pilgrimage to the grave of Robert Burns, a poet with who he is often compared) and England to promote it and conduct readings in 1891.

Back home the next year Riley resumed his lecture and reading tour, teaming up with millionaire author Douglass Sherley for a hugely successful double bill. Coinciding with this, in a savvy and astute cross-promotion, Riley compiled and published perhaps his best-loved book, *Rhymes of Childhood*. It's a work that continues to be popular into the 21$^{st}$ century. It also parted the beginning of the end for Riley's literary reputation. Although he continued to sell out readings in New York and across the US (in fact prospective audience members were often turned away), critics increasingly found his work repetitive and banal. His 1894 verse volume *Armazindy* was very poorly received.

Riley gave his last tour in 1895 and spent his final years in Indianapolis writing patriotic poetry for public recitation on civic occasions (with stirring titles such as *America!* and *The Name of Old Glory*) and poem/elegies for famous friends. His life's work of essays, poems, plays and articles was published in sixteen volumes in 1914.

By this time, Riley was in poor health, weakened by years of heavy drinking. The Hoosier Poet died on July 23, 1916 of a stroke. In a final, unusual tribute, Riley lay in state for a day in the Indiana Statehouse, where thousands came to pay their respects. Not since Lincoln had a public personage received such a send-off. He is buried at Crown Hill Cemetery in Indianapolis.

Riley's legacy is not just a literary one. A wealthy man, he left behind the funding seeds for a number of memorial projects, the James Whitcomb Riley Hospital for Children, Camp Riley for children with disabilities and James Whitcomb Riley House (a museum in which the writer's personal effects and furnishings from his lifetime remain unchanged).

And, as a lasting tribute, the town of Greenfield holds a festival every year in Riley's honor. Every October the "Riley Days" festival opens with a flower parade in which local school children place flowers around the statue of Riley set on the courthouse lawn.

Remembered as both a philanthropist and a poet laureate for the Hoosier state of Indiana, a writer with a distinctive pre-industrial folk ethos and an ear for the humble rhythms of the plain local dialect of the US Midwest, Riley remains to this day a poet of the people.

www.ingramcontent.com/pod-product-compliance
Lightning Source LLC
Chambersburg PA
CBHW071327040426
42444CB00009B/2105